DIFFERENCE
AND
DIFFICULTY:

INSIGHTS, ISSUES AND DILEMMAS

Edited by:

Len Barton and Felicity Armstrong

UNIVERSITY OF SHEFFIELD
DEPARTMENT OF EDUCATIONAL STUDIES

Title first published 1999

University of Sheffield
Department of Educational Studies
388 Glossop Road
Sheffield
S10 2JA

ISBN: 0 902831 37 2

Acknowledgements

Editorial Board

Felicity Armstrong
Derrick Armstrong
Elaine Millard
Cathy Nutbrown
Jerry Wellington

The editors would like to thank Helen Oliver for her help, support and patience in the production of this book.

In addition, the editors wish to thank Martin Fenwick for his assistance in printing this publication.

The editors wish to thank the OECD for permission to use four tables from the OECD publication (1995) 'Integrating students with special needs into mainstream schools'.

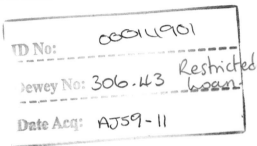

CONTENTS   Page

PREFACE

INCLUSIVE EDUCATION RESEARCH CENTRE

Members:

*Derrick Armstrong, Felicity Armstrong, Len Barton,
Peter Clough, Michele Moore*

This book has developed from ideas and discussions by members of the centre. It is the first in a series of books that we intend to publish.

Responses to the book will be most welcome. Contact can be made through Helen Oliver, email: h.j.oliver@sheffield.ac.uk

5

CONTRIBUTORS

Derrick Armstrong, *Department of Educational Studies, University of Sheffield, 388 Glossop Road, SHEFFIELD S10 2JA, UK.*

Felicity Armstrong, *Department of Educational Studies, University of Sheffield, 388 Glossop Road, SHEFFIELD S10 2JA, UK.*

Len Barton, *Department of Educational Studies, University of Sheffield, 388 Glossop Road, SHEFFIELD S10 2JA, UK.*

Hazel Bines, *Faculty of Health, Social Work & Education, University of Northumbria, Coach Lane Campus, NEWCASTLE UPON TYNE NE7 7XA, UK.*

Peter Clough, *Department of Educational Studies, University of Sheffield, 388 Glossop Road, SHEFFIELD S10 2JA, UK.*

Jenny Corbett, *Institute of Education, University of London, 25 Woburn Square, LONDON WC1H 0AA, UK.*

Gillian Fulcher, *Lares Green, 9 The Ridge, Mount Eliza, Victoria 3930, Australia.*

Roger Slee, *Graduate School of Education, University of Western Australia, Nedlands, Perth, WA 6009, Australia.*

Chris Winter, *Department of Educational Studies, University of Sheffield, 388 Glossop Road, SHEFFIELD S10 2JA, UK.*

INTRODUCTION

LEN BARTON & FELICITY ARMSTRONG

The Units in this book constitute part of the Difference and Difficulty Module which is part of the distance learning, part-time M.Ed Course in Inclusive Education. Our intention in producing this material has been to provide students with some of the latest thinking and research on a range of significant topics which will provide a stimulus for further work and exploration.

We have been encouraged to produce this in book form so that other people not undertaking the course may have access to the material. For such readers the set readings for each activity have been clearly identified and can be followed up.

These Units do not represent the final and authoritative voice on these topics, nor is their approach to the issues, questions or explorations a unified one. The authors are at different stages of development with regard to their experience, understanding, commitment and willingness to take risks over the nature of their interpretations and basic visions. Also, given the complexity of the issues and the limitation of the wordage for each Unit, the authors have provided a series of selective insights and questions dealing with their topics. Much more could have been presented, needs to be followed up and has yet to be developed.

The authors do have some basic points of commonalty underpinning their perspectives. They recognise that how 'difference' is conceived in society, by whom, why and with what consequences, is of fundamental importance. They believe it is essential to identify and understand those factors that make 'difference' so significant, that oppression, exclusion and discrimination become basic features of the social relations and conditions of a society. They agree that this is not merely an individual or attitudinal problem but one that has become institutionalised and part of the inequalities and social divisiveness of a society. Thus for them, like Clarke and Saraga (1998), these definitions and decisions arise from the ways in which we think about the social world and are "...not natural, inevitable, or intrinsic to the people being so described" (p.1).

Whilst all the authors are involved in research on disability issues, they agree that the question of difference goes beyond the concerns with disablement. It is ultimately about the identification and removal of all forms of oppression and the realisation of a society in which inclusion, equity and the celebration of difference with dignity are fundamental values. Yet, the authors also recognise that basic concepts and ideas are contestable and need to be struggled over. This will in varying degrees be a disturbing, difficult and exciting process.

Both in terms of their own development and that of students they agree that learning must get beyond instrumental interests, such as status, marks or a means to a job, and begin to address issues of self-identity and personal empowerment. Of necessity this entails engaging self-critically with personal values, existing forms of knowledge and understanding.

In approaching the reading of these Units it is essential to think about the issues, insights, questions raised in a **relational** manner. Establishing connections between perspectives is a very difficult but vitally significant element in effective learning. The links are by no means straightforward and will often involve contradictory and confusing aspects. Nevertheless, the benefits are worthwhile.

It is also important to recognise the value of an **historical** understanding of those crucially important issues. How policies and practices have changed within and across particular periods of history hopefully helps us not to reinvent the wheel, as well as understanding that 'difference' and 'disability' have meant different things in different historical periods and cultural contexts and thus are amenable to change.

Finally, we hope you will engage with the reading of this book from a developing appreciation that we are always and ever **learners**. Thus, there is no place for arrogance or complacency in the privileged opportunity and process of seeking to develop an informed awareness, including one's own limitations, but one which makes a difference in our lives and hopefully others with whom we interact and work.

REFERENCES

Clarke, J. & Saraga E. (1998) Introduction in Saraga, E. (Ed) *Embodying the social: constructions of difference,* London: Routledge.

UNIT ONE

HISTORIES OF INCLUSION: PERSPECTIVES ON THE
HISTORY OF SPECIAL EDUCATION
DERRICK ARMSTRONG

INTRODUCTION

It is argued in this Unit that the special education system has been the product of competing and often contradictory policy discourses. In the UK these discourses have comprised a humanitarian policy discourse of 'inclusion' which has called for the extension of educational opportunities to all alongside a contradictory policy discourse of focusing on academic standards and the normalisation of academic achievement. The contention of this Unit is that these contradictory policy discourses have provided the backdrop against which practical struggles over the meaning and purpose of education have been carried out. The conflict between these two discourses is contextualized within the processes of wider socio-political struggles and circumstances and it is in relation to these contexts that practical struggles over 'enacted' policy take place (Fulcher, 1989).

In this Unit we consider how history is contested not only in the struggles that are recorded but also in the voices that are represented in its telling. It goes on to review how 'otherness' and exclusion have been created through the system of categorisation that has developed in the UK. Categorisation has itself embodied contradictory policy discourses, in that while providing the basis for exclusion it has also historically been the vehicle through which resources have been redistributed to children to whom education has been denied. Finally the Unit returns to the question of: 'Whose history?' and uses life-history data to illustrate the crucial significance of insider perspectives.

WHOSE HISTORY IS THIS?

Special Education systems are to be found in most parts of the world. Wherever there is an education system there has almost inevitably arisen up alongside it a special education system for children with 'learning difficulties' of different kinds and for disabled children. Many people would argue that there is a need for even more 'special educational services' but when arguments are put forward for the latter it is not always the same thing that is being argued for as that provided by a special education system. This distinction is an important one. Many children experience considerable learning difficulties in their education. Children would doubtless benefit from teachers who are trained and prepared to work with the complexity of different learning needs and who are supported in their work by colleagues with particular expertise and skills. Yet it is also the case that children's learning difficulties are often not dealt with appropriately because of inadequacies in school organisation and the delivery of services and because teachers are inadequately prepared to work with the needs of ALL children. A special education system may at best be a bureaucratic response to needs that are unmet. More often it has arisen out of policies for sorting and discarding those considered to be 'useless' in the modern world.

Understanding this distinction is of crucial importance for arguments against special systems of education but does not in any sense imply that there should be an abandonment by educators of those children who experience difficulty within the ordinary classroom. Quite the opposite; the argument is rather that the focus should be shifted on to those aspects of policy and practice that deny educational opportunities and towards a professionalism in teaching that respects difference, values diversity and supports the empowerment of all learners.

I open this Unit by drawing this important distinction for two reasons. The first is that there is a danger in considering the history of 'special education' that this is based upon the a-historical assumption that the study of systems equates to the study of 'needs'. Yet these are not the same. The struggle of educators for the development of identification and assessment procedures to support real learning, along with training in pedagogy has often been, and continues to be, a struggle against enormous odds, but it is a historical struggle that is rarely alluded to – a hidden history. On the other hand the development of systems of classification, categorisation and exclusion tell a quite different history. This is a history that has become part of our common sense assumptions about what 'special education' is.

ACTIVITY ONE

- **Think about your own education.**
- **In what ways would you describe this in terms of inclusion and in what ways in terms of exclusion?**
- **In what ways is the education system different today and what ways is it similar to that described by your own experience?**

CATEGORIES AND THE CREATION OF 'OTHERNESS'

Forms of special care for the 'disabled', the 'ill' and the 'insane' are not recent developments. An illustration of this is provided by the term 'cretin' which is a derivative of the French word 'chretien' (Christian) and is testimony to the fact that in earlier times severely handicapped people were cared for by religious communities. Of course there is also much evidence to suggest that attitudes to life in pre-industrial societies differed in significant ways from those that are familiar today. A lack of sentimentality about life was perhaps born out of the harsh conditions of many, but by no means all, pre-industrial societies. There are certainly examples of the way in which the treatment of disabled people would be judged harsh and inhuman by the moral 'standards' of western Europe today (although, in practice, examples of such inhumanity abound in those societies). Yet, there are also examples of the social inclusion of disabled people in pre-industrial societies once the rigours of birth and infancy had been survived, or when impairments were acquired later in life. Foucault (1967), for example, describes how from the middle ages to the end of the 18th century 'insanity' and 'idiocy' were a part of everyday life, and 'fools and mad men walked the streets'.

By the mid 19th century the industrialising discipline of the factory system in much of Europe had led to the 'mad' and the 'defective' being perceived as a threat to the new social order and consequently requiring confinement and treatment. The social and cultural organisation of European societies was transformed by capitalism and with this came the confinement of the 'poor', the 'unemployed' and the 'defective' in separate institutions where the 'useless' were forced to labour for their keep.

As the 19th century moved on the technology of regulation became increasingly sophisticated in the fine detail of discrimination and separation of different categories of 'uselessness' and the methods of maximising the degree of their 'usefulness' for each. In England, the 19th century saw the introduction of a number of 'reforms' concerned with the identification of particular 'defective' groups and their removal into separate, 'specialist' institutions for isolation or treatment or remediation, depending upon the particular 'deficit' that had been identified. Thus, the introduction of asylums for 'defective' poor children removed these 'troublesome' children from the workhouses; the Idiots Act of 1886 introduced a distinction between 'lunatics' and 'idiots' providing for the placement of 'idiots' in a separate registered hospital or institution; the sub-class of 'imbeciles' was recognised as a group less defective than idiots; and, attention began to be given to the identification of a further group of 'high-grade defectives' or 'feeble-minded' children. By the end of the 1880s the 'feeble-minded' were regarded as an educational and economic problem and the notion that special schooling for this group would benefit the state was one that was formally recognised by the Elementary Education (Defective and Epileptic Children) Act 1899.

14

ACTIVITY TWO

Read Tomlinson's (1985) 'The Expansion of Special Education'. Jot down some notes on the following questions:

1. To what extent do you think the technologies of identification and 'treatment' represented 'advances' in medicine or psychology and to what extent do you think they were themselves the product of wider forms of social reorganisation?

2. What evidence does Tomlinson present to support her argument that the humanitarian rhetoric that insists "all children have special needs" has obscured the real outcomes of the special education system?

CONTRADICTION AND CONSENSUS IN THE GROWTH OF STATE EDUCATION IN ENGLAND

In England the rise of the special school, and therefore of a distinct and separate system of education for children with physical or sensory impairments and/or 'mentally handicapped' and/or 'maladjusted', has been closely linked to the expansion of the state's role as the major educational provider. Yet the provision of state education in England has always been highly contested. It would be misleading to see the development of the system as guided by one purpose, and likewise special education has been the context of a similar range of contested perspectives and interests.

The origins of the state education system cannot be adequately explained solely by reference to the expansion of education and training opportunities in response to economic needs or demands for social reform. Alongside the 'reformist' strand in educational advocacy, the state system has also traditionally played a very significant role in maintaining distinctions of social class, gender and, through the hierarchies of prestige and power based upon 'ability'. The poor were to be trained to be orderly productive members of society (Hurt, 1988).

The apparent contradiction between these is not as great as it may first seem. There is only a contradiction here if we understand the State and its institutions as representing a homogenous body of interests. In practice, however, the State may actually be better described as 'a hegemonic compromise'. What this means is that within the State there are different and sometimes contradictory interests. Moreover, in its actions the State stands in a particular but variable historical relationship to the broader 'civil society', which itself comprises multiple interests. Although the State can rule by sheer force, this is difficult to sustain within modern societies over a protracted period. Power is more efficiently exercised through a consensus that embodies dominant social interests. It is in the struggle over hegemonic control that compromises between different social interests are made and which reconstruct contradictions as consensus in our socio-political experience. Consensus is not so much about agreement as it is about historical compromises.

The incorporation of working class children into a system of education, codified and controlled by dominant social interests and articulated through the machinery of the State, was an outcome of enormous significance. Of course there were those who resisted the introduction of compulsory education on the grounds that it would educate the poor to oppose their masters. By contrast there were those, like the Chartists, who advocated the expansion of compulsory education with precisely this hope in mind. At each stage of its introduction and expansion the policy of compulsory education represented an important compromise between these and other social interests.

THE EXPANSION OF SPECIAL EDUCATION IN ENGLAND

It would be far-fetched indeed to see the introduction of a segregated system of education for disabled children and children with learning difficulties as taking place independently from the rapid expansion of the state provided education system. The development of a segregated 'special' system of education in the United Kingdom was undoubtedly influenced by both humanitarian reformers and eugenicists. Yet the influence of these perspectives must be seen within the overall context of developments within the general system of education.

The introduction of compulsory elementary schooling brought many children into the education system for the first time, children who had previously been excluded or who had excluded themselves. By the 1880s the assumptions (embodied in a 'Code' which governed a system of 'payment by results', strictly specifying the progress of children at different stages) were being increasingly challenged by the presence in school of children who did not achieve the expected standards. As one London school inspector reported at that time:

'Out of every seventy children, twenty-five
were entirely ignorant, they misbehaved,
learned nothing and truanted.'
Quoted in Pritchard 1963, p.117

This brought into question the 'effectiveness' of individual schools (though not, until, much later, the Code itself) with negative consequences for the funding of those schools deemed to be 'failing'.

Under the regime of accountability imposed by the Code, the response to diversity was exclusion. However, in defining the criteria that would lead to exclusion an increasingly 'scientific' approach was adopted, based on an understanding of 'normality'. For example, W.W. Ireland (1877) suggested a twelve-fold delineation of 'idiocy' which included such sub-divisions of ineducable child as the 'genetous', the 'microcephalic', the 'eclampsic', the 'traumatic', the 'inflammatory' and so on.

There was a growing preoccupation with the differentiation of 'mental deficiency' during the latter part of the nineteenth century, originating out of concerns over the ineducability of children *in terms of the Code* (Sutherland, 1984). These concerns led the Royal Commission on the Feeble-minded (the Egerton Commission), set up in 1886, to recommend a principle of differentiation that has been a part of the English system down to the present day. This was based upon a division between mild, moderate and severe learning difficulties with different forms of provision being seen as appropriate for these different groups.

The refinement in classification systems of 'defective' groups must be seen in the context of wider socio-economic and political change. The industrialisation of the economy and the attendant urbanisation of social life that characterised nineteenth century England led to the 'discovery' of the 'mental defective' and a eugenicist drive to control defective populations in the interests of social progress.

The eugenicist Goddard (1914) for instance, recognised that what was seen as constituting 'mental deficiency' in society was very different at different historical periods. Nonetheless, he held the view that it was social and economic 'progress' that revealed the deficiencies of 'moral, physical and mental degenerates'.

> '....the persons who constitute our social problems are of a type that in the past and under simpler environments have seemed responsible and able to function normally, but for whom the present environment has become too complex so that they are no longer responsible for their actions'.
>
> Goddard, 1914, pp 2-3

For Goddard, the growing complexity of social life created conditions under which greater numbers of people had no 'usefulness':

> 'The feeble-minded person is not desirable, he is a social encumbrance, often a burden to himself. In short it were better for him and for society had he never been born'
>
> Goddard, 1914, p 558

Writing from a more 'enlightened' perspective some 20 years later, Duncan (1938:87-8) argued that

'Segregation of feeble-minded children into special schools and the development of a narrow curriculum based on vocational and sub-vocational lines completely different in principle from a curriculum suitable for normal children have led to a view, held in the past, that feeble-minded children have educational requirements quite different from those of normal children, and to an accent on the 'special' … [However, the real problem is that of] fitting education to the differing capacities and needs of all children. The same principles are sound for all.'

Yet, in failing to problematise the social conditions in which differences are reconstructed as deficiencies, Duncan's philosophy of educational inclusion is distinguishable from Goddard's only by the moral position of 'care' that is adopted towards those 'unfortunates' whose 'feeble-mindedness' has been revealed by 'social progress':

'Economic, social and educational changes that have been taking place during the last few years have revealed mental deficiency as a problem of greater magnitude than it was at one time thought to be. People suffering from a great degree of mental defect – idiots and imbeciles – have for centuries been recognised as mental cases. Such cases, however, constitute only a small minority of the total number of mental defectives. The very great majority are the higher grade - feeble-minded – type, many of whom are of normal physical appearance. In years gone by these were not obvious, did not present any very great economic or social problem. Many of them earned a living as "hewers of wood and drawers of water". They helped with agricultural work or with garden work, or in factories doing unskilled manual work often requiring chiefly physical strength. In recent

> years mechanisation of industry and the
> changing nature of agriculture and horticulture
> in this country, due to improved world
> diminished and diminishing demand for
> unskilled labour. Dislocation of industries and
> the changing material needs of a population
> may result in a pool of unemployed labour,
> but a general change throughout all industry,
> such as mechanisation, tends to result in a
> pool of unemployable labour. Changing
> industrial conditions have thus given rise to
> problems of unemployment and have focused
> attention on the existing large number of
> feeble-minded and intellectually dull.'
>
> Duncan, 1938, pp 2-3

The logic of this argument is quite interesting. In the absence of any critique of what constitutes 'progress' it would seem to follow that before too long all but the most intelligent will be useless and therefore eventually categorised as feeble-minded. The inevitability of these changes is simply assumed but at the very least questions are raised about what criteria are being used to evaluate progress.

Duncan's rhetoric of inclusion is trapped within a series of assumptions about the social world and the nature of economic development that lead him to treat the role of the education system as being to respond to the different needs of children as these are 'discovered' or made apparent through the increasing complexity of industrial organisation. He firstly neglects to consider ways in which the education system might itself produce 'needs'; secondly how these 'needs' might be related to the interests of other groups (for instance, the changing role of professionals).

ACTIVITY THREE

Write down in your own words the main arguments that are put forward by Goddard and Duncan in these passages. List what you consider to be the main differences and similarities between the two. In what ways does your own view of 'inclusion' differ from that advanced by Duncan?

It is interesting to compare Duncan's argument with the much later 'discovery' by the Warnock Committee (1978) of 18 per cent of children with 'special educational needs' within the mainstream school. We could see this as reflecting a concern about the academic failure of large numbers of children within the mainstream sector, and therefore as representing a critique of the school system, contributing to the work or early school effectiveness researchers (Rutter et al, 1978). On the other hand, it is hardly unimportant that this discovery was revealed in the wake of the raising of the school leaving age to 16 and at a time when there was a growing crisis of youth unemployment accompanied by concerns about delinquency and social disaffection. In the context of an enforced extension of compulsory education for young people who neither wanted it nor benefited from it, together with restricted employment opportunities, the educational label of 'special needs' conveniently legitimated the educational and socio-economic disadvantages experienced by young people. It embodies an ideology of individual (child or school) failure that delegitimates wider political critique. (Tomlinson, 1988)

It is important that the wider socio-political context of special educational policy is properly recognised. This wider context allows us to cut through the rhetoric of policy frameworks. For example, in a discussion of special education policy in the UK in the early part of the twentieth century, Sutherland (1984:157) noted how 'In the bleak economic climate prevailing after 1918' plans to introduce special schooling for all 'mentally defective' children between the ages of seven and seventeen under the Mental Deficiency Act of 1913 and the Elementary Education (Defective and Epileptic Children) Act, 1914

> 'came to look more and more like extravagant fantasies. Lack of money drove the Board of Education first to re-appraise the role of special schools and then to cease positively to campaign for them'

The irony here is that special schooling for the 'mentally defective' had been proposed as a measure to extend educational opportunities. The abandonment of this policy in the years following the First World War was justified on the grounds that improved methods of identifying educational needs and matching teaching strategies to needs made it more practical to include 'mentally defective' children within the ordinary school. The reality was that large numbers of children continued to be excluded from any form of schooling.

The Wood Committee which reported in 1929 estimated that approximately 18 per cent of children were either 'mentally defective' or 'mentally retarded'. It was argued that the existing special schools were catering for no more than one-sixth of the former group and none of the latter group. It was proposed that the certification of the 'feeble-minded' should be ended so that the 'feeble-minded' and the 'retarded' could be catered for in one comprehensive system. Although the recommendations of the Wood Committee were not incorporated into legislation until the 1944 Education Act made provisions for the education of all but the most seriously 'subnormal', the moves to extend the special school system cannot be understood simply in terms of the exclusion of troublesome children from the ordinary school. It was an 'inclusionary' project, although the underlying organisational principle was that of separate systems for different needs. In this respect the development of special education was consistent with general educational thinking about separate forms of schooling for children of different abilities. As was the case in respect of the ordinary system the attempt to promote inclusion through a separate form of provision ignored contradictions which lay outside the school system and broader society. In so far as it was an ideal, it was an ideal that was unattainable, as was the tripartite ideal of 1944, because of the failure to recognise how the education system operates not only to promote empowerment through learning but also to perpetuate existing privileges, advantages and systems of power.

UNDERSTANDING THE EXPERIENCE OF HISTORY FROM DIFFERENT PERSPECTIVES

It would be misleading to represent the history of special education either in terms of an enlightened movement towards 'progress', 'inclusion' or in simplistic terms of social exclusion and oppression.

The 1981 Education Act has been represented as marking a significant break with the dominant medical model of 'special needs'. Yet, this view ignores continuities in special educational policy in the UK which can be traced back through the Wood Committee Report (Board of

Education, 1929) and, before that, to debates around the 1913 Mental Deficiency Act. These continuities lay in the emphasis upon 'educability' rather than a medical definition of 'deficiency' as the criteria for inclusion within the education system. However, the impacts of these policy formulations did not occur within a vacuum. The post-war recession provided a significant context for the re-negotiation of official policy evidenced, for instance, by the fact that despite official policy, the numbers of 'mentally defective' children placed in special schools between 1914 and 1939 increased by no more than 4000.

Stephen Ball has argued that policies

> "are representations which are encoded in complex ways (via struggles, compromises, authoritative public interpretations and reinterpretations) and decoded in complex ways (via actors' interpretations and meanings in relation to their history, experiences, skills, resources and context) ... [Yet] only certain influences and agendas are recognised as legitimate" 1994:16

Yet, policy analysts who have moved away from an exclusive focus upon the voices of 'official' policy-makers, nonetheless, largely do not engage with the voices of the recipients of special education. It is important that we ask the question: 'whose history is being talked about when we talk of the history of special education?' Once we ask this question we start to understand better the importance of historical analysis for action in the present. If we ask 'whose history?' we start to realise firstly that history is not simply a set of facts about the world but is rather a set of contested perspectives, and secondly that some of those perspectives or voices are left out of official or dominant representations of the story altogether.

Among the voices that are rarely heard are those of people who have experienced 'special education'. Judith Okely (1996) has argued that the exploration of individual stories does not imply that individuals can be seen as self-contained, nor should it lead researchers to minimise the impact of determining structures which, in the last instance, ensure subordination. However, it is through the very a-typicality of individuals, marginalized groups and apparently incidental moments that critical, alternative perspectives on power are offered. Life-history research and its focus on individual stories challenges the homogeneity of experience and resistance and in doing so challenges the relations of power that structurally construct 'otherness' into categories of oppression.

One example of this is suggested by the following extracts from Stanley's life-story (Armstrong, 1998).

Stanley was taken into a Children's Home following the death of his parents when he was only young. Shortly after this he was assessed as 'retarded', denied any sort of education and transferred into the care of a hospital. This would have been approximately 40 years ago and would probably have followed his ascertainment as severely educationally subnormal. In the hospital,

> 'It was all men. All hospital beds. Cold. Right in the most bleak part. Right up on the moors. They used to lock the doors. They used to lock people in and I didn't like it'.

The institution not only defined who he was, i.e. 'retarded' and 'useless', but also obliterated all other possibilities:

> 'I can't remember things when I was in them places. I've lost all remembering'.

When Stanley talks here of 'remembering' he is not talking literally of his memories of the past but rather of the stripping away of his human identity. It soon becomes apparent when working with people who have been labelled as having 'learning difficulties' how significant are the concepts of 'space' and 'time' to the social construction of their 'difference'. Time, for instance, may be understood as a powerful normalising artefact. The label of 'learning difficulties' has constructed the experience of those so labelled as outside the configurations of time and space that are taken for granted by those to whom such a label is not attached. It is only when Stanley, in his 50s, has broken free from the totalising experience of confinement that his 'memory' comes alive:

> "It's only since I've lived here (his own house) that I can remember things. I couldn't even read and write but now I can and I'm doing ever so great with jobs like reading and writing and going to college. I've got a flat. I've got a key of my own which means I can go out and I can go shopping and I'm quite happy with what I'm doing and when I'm on my own I can concentrate, you know like reading and writing".

ACTIVITY FOUR

Read the article by Sparkes, A. (1994) 'Life Histories and the issue of voice: reflections on an emerging relationship'.

What do you understand by the difference between 'life-story' and 'life history'?

Take the extracts from Stanley's story and map out how you might use this sort of data to begin a wider analysis of special education. For instance, what sort of questions does it suggest? What lines of further enquiry might you pursue both through life history research and other forms of historical research?

The life-stories of people educated in the segregated special education sector contest, in practice, the official policy discourses of 'inclusion' that have exerted influence since 1944 in particular. They do so insofar as they illustrate how the experience of special education throughout this period has 'marked' them with a label of exclusion that is carried into later life. They illustrate, in particular, how the special school sector operates as a mechanism by which social, economic and political disadvantage is constructed as 'disability' and the distribution of social rewards and social justice is legitimated through representations of 'disability'.

These stories also emphasise the importance of contextualizing education policy texts within the much broader arena of social policy negotiations and impacts (Armstrong, 1998). Taken in isolation, a policy agenda of 'inclusion' based upon the 'special needs' of those "for whom the present environment has become too complex" (Goddard, 1914) may be continually reconstituted, or rediscovered, in new forms but with essentially the same substantive limitations. The stories of those who have experienced special education illustrate the complex ways in which this experience is tied into the construction and management of 'uselessness'.

CONCLUSION

Policy and provision for special education are frequently cast within a framework which ignores the historical context within which that policy and provision has developed. In so doing there is a tendency to focus upon the child and his or her needs in ways that ignore how those needs have been constructed through the interplay between the education system and wider social, economic and political processes and conditions. This is very apparent in the influence of medical, psychological and managerial perspectives upon the development of special education. Medical and psychological perspectives have emphasised the individuality of need and in so doing easily slip into a theory of needs based upon the deficits of the child. The social context within which the child is situated is treated as unproblematic. Instead, medical and psychological perspectives have informed policy and practice interventions that have centred upon either the 'treatment' of the 'abnormal' child with the 'special' child's behaviour and achievement defined in relation to the requirements of the dominant system of social values and norms. Managerial perspectives have moved beyond the individual child but have still been constrained by a focus upon intervention at the school level which does not adequately account for the relationship between the school system and the social world through which educational policy and provision are given meaning.

In this unit we have looked at how a historical perspective illuminates the contested values and interests that have been struggled over in the growth of the special education sector in the UK. It has been argued that special education policy has been informed by contradictory policy discourses: on the one hand, servicing the mainstream sector by containing those deemed to be unmanageable; on the other hand, providing a mechanism for redistributing resources to children otherwise denied access to an education. For instance, the category of 'severe learning difficulties' was used up to the 1970s to legitimate the denial of education to children so labelled, yet it was through the extension of the special education sector that educational resources and opportunities were eventually made accessible to these children.

It has been further argued that special educational policy can only be meaningfully understood by reference to wider social, economic and political processes of change. 'Inclusion' is not an abstract principle but is a policy discourse that is politically defined at specific historical moments. Thus, as taken up by the disability movement it can articulate a socio-political critique of oppression, whilst in other contexts it may articulate policies of economic retrenchment and political normalisation.

The weakness of much policy analysis appertaining to special education has lain in the manner in which 'handicap' and 'special needs' have been applied. Historical analysis needs to take the voices of disabled people seriously, for they challenge both the homogeneity of experience and the social relations that construct the oppression of 'otherness'. We have begun to explore the significance both of this experience of special education and its implicit articulation of new theoretical understandings of the politics of exclusion and inclusion. This is a theme to which we will frequently return in the units of this Module.

REFERENCES

Armstrong, D. (1998) *The life histories of people with learning difficulties*. (Final Report to the Economic and Social Research Council) Swindon: ESRC.

Ball, S. (1994) *Education Reform: A critical and post-structural approach*, Buckingham: Open University Press.

Board of Education (1929) *Report of the Mental Deficiency Committee* (the Wood Committee), London: Board of Education.

Duncan (1938) *Mental Deficiency*, London: Watts & Co.

Foucault, M. (1967) *Madness and Civilisation: A history of insanity in the age of reason,* London: Tavistock.

Fulcher, G. (1989) *Disabling Policies,* London: Falmer Press.

Goddard, H. H. (1914) *Feeble-Mindedness: Its Causes and Consequences*, New York: Macmillan.

Hurt, J. (1988) *Outside the Mainstream: A History of Special Education,* London: Routledge.

Ireland, W.W. (1877) *On Idiocy and Imbecility*, London: J & A. Churchill.

Okely, J. (1996) *Own or Other Culture*, London: Routledge.

Pritchard, D. G. (1963) *Education and the Handicapped 1760-1960*, London: Routledge and Kegan Paul.

Rutter, M., Maughn, B., Mortimore, P., Ouston, J. and Smith, A. (1979) *Fifteen Thousand Hours: Secondary Schools and their Effects on Pupils*, London: Open Books.

Sparkes, A. (1994) 'Life histories and the issue of voice: reflections on an emerging relationship' in *Qualitative Studies in Education*, Vol 1, No 2, pp 165-183.

Sutherland, G. (1984) *Ability, Merit and Measurement: Mental Testing and English Education 1880 - 1940*, Oxford: Clarendon Press.

Tomlinson, S. (1985) 'The expansion of special education' in *Oxford Review of Education*, Vol 11, No 2, pp 157-165.

Tomlinson, S. (1988) 'Why Johnny can't read: critical theory and special education' in *European Journal of Special Needs Education*, No 3, pp 45 - 58.

Warnock, M. (1978) *Special Educational Needs*, London: HMSO

UNIT TWO

POLICY CONCERNS

GILLIAN FULCHER

INTRODUCTION

This unit asks you to consider the nature of policy. It offers a *political -* or socio-political - perspective on policy: that makes it different from *policy analysis* . It shows, through examining various policy documents, the range of *social actors* (individuals or groups) who engage in making policy *at all levels* of a *state apparatus* such as education.

It discusses definitions of disability: how these vary between groups, even though some of these groups may have the same political objectives. Here it raises, briefly, the problem of impairment: how some use the term interchangeably with disability, a view others contest.

The unit examines the ideas of rights, inclusive education and special educational needs also from a political perspective

The section *Policy Concerns* raises briefly the context of education policy, especially the importance of the language that politicians/educators/public servants tend to deploy. It discusses the use of a *rational discourse* in policy and its current substantive themes such as effectiveness, etc.; it also refers to the notion of *principles for policy,* as well as the absence of any reference to *power* or *politics* or *morality* in this policy discourse.

Corporate culture - or market thinking - and its language - which has overtaken public discourse - is also outlined, as is its emphasis on individuals. The consequences of this habit of thought are briefly referred to.

You are asked to analyse one or two documents for their language: for the actions they imply and the objectives they reveal.

Finally, the questions of disability, race and gender in policy are posed. These debates are complex but crucial.

A NOTE ON AUSTRALIAN GOVERNMENT LEVELS

There are three levels of government in Australia: The Commonwealth (Federal), State and Local. All three interact in complex ways.

There are six States: New South Wales, Queensland, South Australia, Tasmania, Victoria and West Australia. Three of these States have acronyms: N.S.W., S.A., and W.A. The two most populous States are N.S.W. (where Captain Cook arrived in 1788) and Victoria; they account for about half the overall population of some 17 million.

In addition to the States, there are two Territories: The Australian Capital Territory (A.C.T.) (built to house Federal Government), and the Northern Territory (N.T.) (where most indigenous Australians live). The Territories have less independence from the Commonwealth government than the States.

The Constitution sets out some of the relations between levels of government. The Commonwealth makes laws which govern (create conditions) for certain areas of State life, and for external relations. The Commonwealth government has two Houses: a House of

Representatives and the Senate. State governments have two chambers: a House of Representatives and an Upper House. Local governments may be called Shires, Councils, or Cities; they have complex responsibilities.

Both the Commonwealth and the States may make laws which affect the same area: for instance, both levels may pass legislation on disability. The Commonwealth and the States have a Commonwealth-State Disability Agreement which has been re-negotiated over some years. Local government has responsibilities in disability: for example, in providing Home and Community Care.

DEFINITIONS

Policy

I. . . . 3. political sagacity; statecraft; diplomacy; in bad sense, political cunning. late ME. (The Shorter Oxford English Dictionary).

What is 'policy'? The quick reply is that 'policy' is a set of statements made in documents or pronouncements. As we shall see, that answer isn't much help analytically. There's a more considered answer which takes us into sociology.

But let's consider 'policy' as though it is merely statements. From experience, we know these statements aren't necessarily 'going to happen': they may be someone's hope or intent; they may or may not carry a clear intent; they are likely to be equivocal, for various reasons.

```
ACTIVITY ONE

(a)   Find, or listen to and transcribe, three statements
about education in general (not inclusive education).
What are the key terms or phrases?   Write notes on
their meanings.   Can you find more than one meaning
for each term?   If so, which groups might hold which
meanings and why?

Do this before you go any further.
```

Rhetoric has a place in political statements: it is central to *political* life: it creates constituencies, it contains agendas, it is meant to draw in its audience, and it seeks to retain 'the initiative' (remain on the front foot) for pursuing its (covert?) political objectives.   Rhetoric wins political debates (in debating societies, on TV shows and in Parliament). But how far does the idea of rhetoric take us analytically? Not far.

Can we bypass that analytical impasse if we think about policy as something governments 'make' and others 'implement'?

The ideas of policy as rhetoric, or as a top-down phenomenon, aren't much help for understanding policy.   We need a socio-political perspective on policy as a *political phenomenon*.

A SOCIO-POLITICAL PERSPECTIVE ON POLICY

As the work of Barry Hindess implies, there is a clear distinction between policy analysis and political theorising.   Thus, as others suggest:

> The critique of policy cannot be done from within the framework that policy has been written. We must stand back from policy to see its shortcomings. We cannot expect to solve problems within existing structures of thought and practice (Branson and Miller, 1989:166).

We can begin to think outside 'existing structures of thought and practice' by exploring the idea that *policy is written at different levels.* Who writes educational policies? Look at the titles of the N.S.W. policy documents and note who wrote them.

Let's begin with the 1996 N.S.W. Integration/Inclusion Feasibility Study. The new N.S.W. Labour Minister for Education and Employment, John Aqualina, commissioned the report from David McRae, an educational consultant from Victoria. The report refers to N.S.W. State government legislation and other policy on disability and education, and to Commonwealth legislation surrounding inclusive education. *(You might want to look at the Note on Levels of Australian government at this point.)* The study contains recommendations for policy development. It appears to be made at a number of levels of government, and in various forms: as legislation, as recommendations, and in other statements. Written policy is clearly complex, *made at various levels and comes in different forms: it consists of different practices such as legislation, report writing, etc (see Hindess, 1986; Fulcher, 1989a: introduction).*

The *Kids Belong Together* policy documents are from a parent group which campaigned widely in 1994, lobbying the then Shadow Minister (Labour) for Education and Training, John Aqualina. The group continues, in 1998, to campaign widely and to issue policies. Campaigning for policy - lobbying a Shadow Minister who subsequently commissions a report in response - reveals *policy as struggle - as involving more than statements - and as a political process.*

These two sets of policy documents show that (written) 'policy' is 'made' at national and other levels of government, and by parent groups and that an educational consultant also makes policy (in the form of advice).

(Administrators - public servants - would deny they make policy but the administrative model of policy talks about policy apolitically: as policy, implementation, outcome.) Each of these groups or individuals - including the consultant? - are *key actors in policy making.*

The Queensland Teacher Union document contains a section on the N.S.W. Union of Teachers: teacher unions then are another key actor in policy struggles. The PLEDG document from W.A. shows that educational consultants may 'make' policy with schools, communities and parents, independent of the W.A. Department of Education or Minister.

Len Barton's 1997 paper comments on the Green Paper 'Excellence for All Children: Meeting Special Educational Needs' (1997). Is this a powerful attempt to influence teacher union policy? Should we add Professors of Education as possible key actors in policy struggles?

In sum, even with a restricted idea of policy as statements, these documents reveal that policy *meanings are contested, policy is complex, it's 'made' at various levels, and by different actors in policy struggles, and that it involves action (for instance, campaigning).*

Saying that policy is struggle means that policy is political. *Politics is contests* (Wickham, cited in Fulcher, 1992). Policy is the *outcome of political states of play, or struggles, in a particular arena: wherever decisions are made* (Fulcher, 1989a). The outcome of contests cannot be guaranteed. 'Politics as contests have no given actors, no given forms and no pre-determined outcomes (Wickham, cited in Fulcher, 1992:6). Policy, at say, a national level may create conditions for policy practices in other arenas at other levels, but it does not determine them (Hindess, 1986). *How important are these insights in understanding government and policy?*

We need to add two dimensions to this socio-political perspective on policy: the first is the idea of *discourse*. Discourse and its institutional bases are at the centre of this framework. Discourse is how we talk about something. The same words (integration, for example) may appear in different discourses: how is a term such as integration deployed in discourse A and differently in discourse B? (See *Vlachou (1997:chapter 4) on teachers' views of integration, and Mousely, Rice & Tregenza (1993).*

Can we better understand a discourse and its politics by identifying its objective? If we identify the objective, we see that the terms in a discourse are deployed to achieve the objective. Our discourse is thus both tactic (Macdonald, 1981), and theory about how that particular aspect of the social world we wish to influence works (Fulcher, 1989a, etc). For instance, we might say, and believe, that this child is integrated in the school (though she's in a special class) and that this is how integration works in this instance. Another teacher might say that that child is segregated.

Our socio-political perspective on policy also needs locating in a wider theory of social relations. Social relations consist of practical projects: whether that's digging a vegetable patch, advancing our career, or raising a child. In each of our projects we struggle to achieve our objectives (these are not necessarily those of self-interest) and in each we deploy discourse.

(See Fulcher (1989a:15 'the model . . . - 16) on this.)

In this framework , policy - whether written, stated or enacted are *social practices* . Legislation, speeches, reports, classroom decisions are all examples of social practices.

This model of social relations as practices has important moral and political implications. All practices are simultaneously *technical* (how something can be done), *moral* (this is how it should be done: here - in the regular classroom, rather than . . .), and *political* (I am able to make - have the power to carry out - that decision).

DISABILITY

Disability is *disputed* (Fulcher, 1989a:24)

Groups struggle over the definition of disability. Why? Because much hinges on it politically, socially, economically: it's at the centre of governmental and other struggles.

How shall we sort our way through the plethora of definitions? It's useful to distinguish an analytical meaning we might use in a socio-political perspective from the substantive meanings which appear in policy and in political campaigns. The difference is subtle, and debatable; sometimes the two merge. But analytical meanings can clarify an area: their objective is to sort out what's going on in these struggles. In contrast, substantive meanings - the meanings I deploy to achieve my objective - whether in policy or in the disability movement or in something else - seek to establish a position and achieve my objective.

Compare the British Council of Disabled People's definitions of impairment and disability (2.3.1), with an Australian policy document (2.3.2), a political analysis (2.3.3), the Australian disability movement's term (2.3.4), and the British disability movement's term (2.3.5):

The British Council of Disabled People's definition:

> ***Disability*** is the disadvantage or restriction of activity caused by a society which takes little or no account of

people who have impairments and thus excludes them from mainstream activity. (Therefore, *disability*, like racism or sexism, is discrimination and social oppression.)

Impairment is a characteristic, feature or attribute within an individual which is long term and may or may not be the result of disease or injury and may

1. affect that individual's appearance in a way which is not acceptable to society, and or

2. affect the function of that individual's mind or body, either because of, or regardless of society, and/or

3. cause pain, fatigue, affect communication and/or reduce consciousness.

Disabled people are those people with *impairments* who are disabled by society .

This distinguishes disability from impairment and provides, some say, the basis for a social model of disability. It says that society disables people with impairments. Some of its proponents do not wish to talk about impairment in these struggles; others do (eg. Jenny Morris).

Definitions in an Australian policy document (Integration/Inclusion...)

'Students with disabilities are defined according to the category of their disability and in some case its level of severity (McRae, 1997:2)

'*Sensory Disabilities*

These definitions come from the *Interim State Procedural Guidelines*..

Vision (V): 'visual impairment that is 6/24 (corrected) . . . ' (McRae, 1997:7)

This muddles disability and impairment and uses them interchangeably. (With what political effects on policy?)

Terms in a socio-political perspective

> Disability is not about wheelchairs . . . Nor is it to be understood as primarily a medical phenomenon . . . Rather, disability is a category which is central to how welfare states regulate an increasing proportion of their citizens. In this sense and context, it is a *political and social construct* used to regulate (Fulcher, 1989:21).

This is an analytical use for a socio-political perspective which does not pronounce what the meaning of disability is. It says (as the text goes on to say later) that disability is a term which is deployed - politically.

The Australian disability movement's definitions

> People with disabilities (Australian disability movement and the term in Australian government policies, including legislation).

This politically held term suggests people have disabilities. This position is at odds with the British Council of Disabled People and with the next definition. Note that Australians with disabilities have ostensibly the same objective as the British Council of Disabled People.

The British disability movement's term

> Disabled people

This implies society disables people. Another meaning is that we are disabled and proud of it - that disabled is also something people have. Clearly the meanings aren't settled once and for all.

ACTIVITY TWO

Read Liggett, H. (1988) 'Stars are not born: an interpretative approach to the politics of disability'.

Liggett argues that the identity of 'disabled' is sometimes useful in struggles and sometimes not. Do you agree? Write notes on your answer. Which of the above groups might oppose you? Might you have the same objective as these groups? What then, is the key difference between you? Write notes on your answer.

RIGHTS

In democracies of the modern west, the assertion of human rights is an important principle. Nations without a democratic tradition also claim a tradition of human rights. The idea of human rights can be deployed in struggles at whatever level, but the outcome of these struggles cannot be guaranteed

> Need is therefore not about privileged provision as Stone (1984) argues: its real politics are about exclusion. The attempt to challenge these politics via a discourse on rights has failed, for instance, in North America and in Victoria. In contrast, the Danish Ministry's focus on pedagogic issues for pupils appears to avoid these politics (Fulcher, 1989b:24)

Increasingly, contending parties now assert rights over an ever-widening range of endeavour.

INCLUSIVE EDUCATION

Politics shift, hence the terms deployed shift. The idea of integration once had a political edge, it seemed, in favour of children marginalized from regular education. The idea of inclusive education may now have that edge: But for how long? Are the struggles around the idea of inclusive education the same as those which surrounded integration?

(See Vlachou, A. 1997, chapter 4, and Fulcher, G. 1989).

SPECIAL EDUCATIONAL NEEDS

Is the idea of special educational needs problematic? And if so, why? What are the range of consequences for individual children? And what are the structural consequences of this term for educational systems? You may wish to *write some notes on your answers to these questions before reading further.*

POLICY CONCERNS

CONTEXT

Governments relate to their historical context by claiming or rejecting, wholly or in part, the tradition of the past. But all governments - however they relate to the past, and to any party tradition - claim a new mandate ('initiatives'). The language shifts as the government's fortunes change. This is an important aspect of the broader context influencing all policy practices. *Politics shifts.*

CONTEXT - LANGUAGE - SUBSTANCE

> To an outstanding degree, politics today is in
> fact conducted in public by means of the
> spoken or written word (Weber, in Gerth &
> Mills, 1974:95)

> *how* language is used matters (Fulcher,
> 1989a:4)

THE LANGUAGE OF RATIONALITY: A RATIONAL

DISCOURSE IN POLICY

The past and present treatment of Aboriginals are at the centre of
Australian politics.   In an essay called 'The Stolen Generations',
Professor Robert Manne asks how it was possible for various policy
makers in Australia, in the 1930s and later, to pursue the policies that
they did.   He finds part of the explanation lies in 'the habit of mind of
key policy-makers'.   He describes this habit of mind as a scientific,
bureaucratic rationality:

> The style of scientific, bureaucratic rationality
> served to shield the key policy-makers from
> the extreme acts of cruelty their policy
> prescriptions inflicted on thousands of human
> beings (Manne, 1998:32).

Since the 1930s, the influence of **rationality** on our thinking - **as a
particular kind of discourse** - has increased.   As the German
sociologist, Max Weber predicted: as bureaucracy increases so does
rationality.[1]

You'll be familiar with the terms in this rational policy discourse:
effective, efficient, cost-effective, choice, strategy, outcome, objective,

---

[1] The rationality of government policy, or of corporate policy may be questioned in the sense
that the ends are non-rational. The ends aside, the means to these ends may be seen as
calculatingly rational. See Weber (1974:115-18) on types of rationality.

goal, implementation, performance, performance indicator, incentive, ethics, procedures, excellence, world's best practice, responsibility, opportunity, etc., and, most importantly, principles.

Here is what one veteran watcher of social policy says on principles in policy:

> Government social policy is not now - and never has been - based on rational analysis or on any one coherent and consistent set of principles. For better or worse, discussions of what principles should determine social provision are not likely to be very productive (Piachaud, 1991).

The problem with policy principles is that they are asserted in the absence of discussing the politics which will allow or prevent their realisation. The rational tale of policy is silent on its politics and morality (Fulcher, 1992:66ff.). Since all practices are simultaneously moral, political and technical, this is a significant (political) omission.

The rational tale of policy masks its politics: it is silent on the contests which surround legislation and other forms of policy practices such as pronouncements, statements, recommendations, reports and decisions in, for instance, classrooms. The word 'appropriate' is often used to evade these politics.

This approach to policy practices - the deployment of a rational discourse - occludes the morality which inheres in every decision (should we teach these students here or there?). The language in the rational tale of policy is thus a tool of control: one government deploys in administering populations.

So the terms 'ethics' and 'principles' encourage those who listen to, or read, policy to take what Shapiro (1988) calls the path of linguistic least resistance. When we see the terms ethics and principles in a policy, we need to think about its morality (ought this to happen, or that? and in whose interest?); and we need to think also about its politics: who will prevail?

MARKET THINKING, CORPORATE CULTURE AND A RATIONAL DISCOURSE - AND ALSO, THE ACADEMY

Market thinking, or economic rationalism, as it is called in Australia - that habit of thought which excludes consideration of social issues - constrains policy makers' thinking. Market thinking is what epitomises corporate culture. The language of **corporate culture** consists of terms like performance, competition, partnership (ironies abound), skill, objective, etc, and above all the notion of consumer: in health, for instance. (The idea of health consumers would have been unthinkable a couple of decades ago). Sometimes policy 'consumers' are called 'customers', as now happens to Australian ratepayers (customers of local government).

Corporate culture, or discourse - the language and life of trade as we currently conduct it - is now so widespread, it has entered two institutions formerly seen as separate from the world of business. It permeates the thinking of government Ministers - hence government policy. It is possible to argue, at least in Australia, especially in Victoria, that government Ministers see no difference between business and governing. This marks a shift in the centuries old democratic project. Secondly, corporate culture has entered the academy. So, in the academy, even if we pretend to an intellectual approach - such as a socio-political perspective on policy - we must make a continuous effort to draw on a vocabulary which isn't that of trade. This effort is difficult because corporate culture - and discourse - permeates everyday life. To take one practice as an instance: corporations now subsidise computers in primary schools.

In the nineties, the style of bureaucratic rationality in government policy has changed from scientific rationality to corporate rationality, though science - a positivist view - remains an influence (hence the policy mania to measure). The underlying drive of rational thinking, however, remains the same: that of mastery, control and calculation: in government's case, of populations and sub-populations. Evidence for this lies in intensified governmental technologies: in its methods of administration. Instances include the use of professional assessment and computerised records. Where disabled students are concerned, individual statements and methods of assessment are just two examples of this increasing rationality.

INDIVIDUALISM

Policy which promotes the idea of people as individuals deploys **an individualistic discourse**. Earlier policy language used terms which thought of people in different - more connected - ways: as 'the public' - so the idea of 'in the public interest' could be deployed in politics - and as citizens. None of these terms have fixed meanings, so the wider discourse in which they appear needs noting. Thus the shift from the classical meanings of the idea of the citizen to the notion of the 'active citizen' occurred in a discourse which differed from the classical notions of democracy.   The individual as the chief character in social life in the 1990s, portrayed as a consumer having choice, is inconsistent with the idea of a democratic community of citizens.

These influences - which I've suggested so far - come from the wider context - rationality, market thinking, corporate culture, and individualism in its latest version of people as consumers - combine in complex ways to influence policy making at all levels.   But the reverse is true: policy influences everyday life.

ACTIVITY THREE

Read DFEE (1997) Excellence for all children: meeting special educational needs.

- **What is its discourse?**

- **Is it individualistic?**

- **Is it medical in its approach to Special Educational Needs?**

- **What problems are there in using a corporate discourse to discuss inclusive education?**

The *language of economic rationalism* (another name for corporate discourse) *has no necessary content or substance.* Its terms such as cost-effective, efficient, objective, goal, performance, performance indicator are abstract terms. Those who deploy the language of economic rationalism present these abstract terms as though there are no dilemmas about what these terms might mean, as though everyone agrees on particular goals. An irony in economic rationalism is that the discourse may capture those who deplore it in others. (Fulcher, 1992:66).

CONCLUSION

The unit outlines a political model of policy. Hence, terms in policy need to be examined as political tactic - as having strategic meanings aimed at particular objectives - rather than as having any inherent, fixed or desirable meaning. This applies as much to ideas like disability, impairment, rights, inclusive education and special education, as it does to more obviously political terms like effectiveness, downsizing, strategy, etc.

The political model of policy has been put forward both in the text and in the six diagrams which follow.

In discussing the idea of rights, the unit has suggested that 'contending parties now assert rights over an ever-increasing range of endeavour' (think of some mad examples); and further, that the outcome of these struggles over rights - whatever their moral ground can not - like the outcome of democracy - be guaranteed.

Inclusive education may be seen as a new political term - new, because politics shift, so terms shift - which may have the same fate as 'integration.' The unit suggests that the idea of special educational needs is difficult politically, and educationally; it cites various authors who've written on the consequences of this category - both for individual children and structurally, for the education.

ACTIVITY FOUR

Consider whether we need to distinguish between analysis and politics. This is not to suggest, of course, that any analysis or research or topic is 'value-free.' It raises the question of a difference between enquiry and political agendas; and, if there is a distinction - however difficult - how important it may be to be clear about the difference - politically not just intellectually.

DIAGRAMS

diagram 1

policy defined:

the outcome of political states

of play in a particular arena

diagram 2

policy at
all levels

policy
'remade'

diagram 3

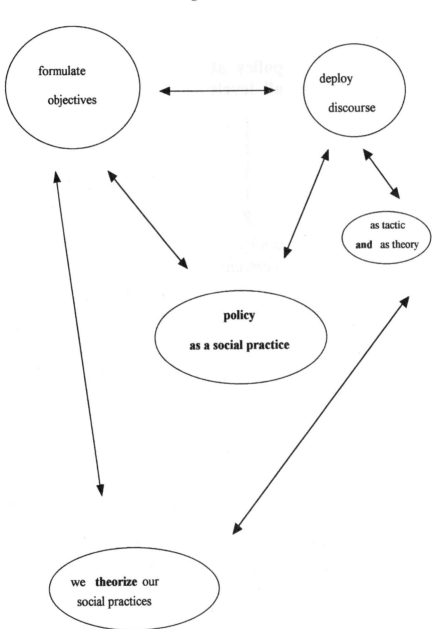

diagram 4

policy - politics

inseparable?

diagram 5

Policy	Political analysis
has 'silences' - what it doesn't talk about:	**has a**
_____	_____
~ power	~ view of power and its workings
~ politics	~ an array of concepts which link power and its bases to its effects
~ morality, except via	~ various theories
'access'	
'equity'	
'dignity'	
'social justice'	

diagram 6

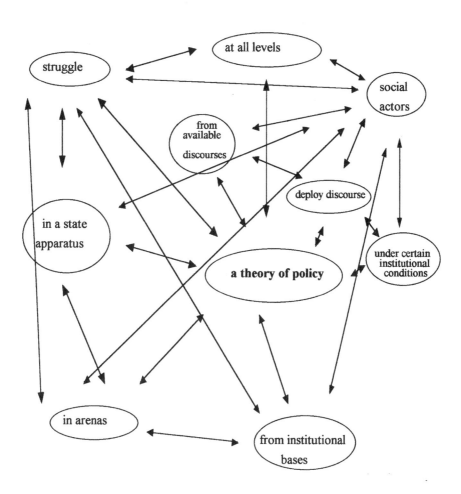

Hindess (1986)
Fulcher (1989)

Fulcher 1989

REFERENCES

Allan, J. (1996) 'Foucault and Special Educational Needs: a "box of tools" for analysing children's experiences of mainstreaming' in *Disability & Society*, Vol 11, No 2, pp 219-33.

Barton, L. (1998) 'Inclusive Education and Human Rights' in *Socialist Teacher*, No 65, Spring, pp 27 - 30.

Branson, J. and Miller, D. (1989) 'Beyond Integration Policy - The Deconstruction of Disability' in Barton, L. (Ed) *Integration: Myth or Reality*, London: The Falmer Press, pp 144 - 67.

Corbett, J. (1997) 'Teaching Special Needs: "tell me where it hurts"' in *Disability & Society*, Vol 12, No 3, pp 417 - 425.

Fulcher, G. (1989a) *Disabling Policies: A comparative approach to education policy and disability*, London: The Falmer Press.

Fulcher, G. (1989b) 'Integrate and Mainstream? Comparative issues in the politics of these policies' in Barton, L. (Ed) *Integration: Myth or Reality*, London: The Falmer Press, pp 6 - 29.

Fulcher, G. (1990) *PICK UP THE PIECES! What do recreation workers need to know about policy and working with people with severe disabilities?* Report prepared for the Department of Leisure and Recreation, Phillip Institute of Technology, Victoria.

Fulcher, G. (1995) 'Excommunicating the Severely Disabled' in Clough, P. and Barton, L. (Eds) *Making Difficulties Research and Construction of SEN*, London: Paul Chapman Publishing Ltd, pp 6 - 24.

Gerth, H.H. & Mills, C. Wright (1974) *From Max Weber: Essays in sociology*, London: Routledge & Kegan Paul.

Hindess, B. (1986) 'Actors and Social Relations' in Wardell, M.L and Turner, S.P. (Eds) *Sociological Theory in Transition,* Boston: Allen & Unwin.

Liggett, H. (1988) 'Stars are not born: an interpretative approach to the politics of disability' in *Disability, Handicap and Society*, Vol 3, No 3, pp 263 - 76.

Macdonald, I. (1981) 'Assessment: a social dimension' in Barton, L. and Tomlinson, S. (Eds) *Special Education: Policies, Practices and Social Issues*, London: Harper & Row.

Manne, R. (1998) 'The Stolen Generations' in Manne, R. *The Way We Live Now: The Controversies of the Nineties,* Melbourne: Text Publishing, pp 15 - 41.

Marks, G. (1994) 'Armed now with hope: the construction of the subjectivity of students within integration' in *Disability & Society*, Vol 9, No 1, pp 71 - 84.

Morris, J. (1992) 'Personal and Political: A feminist perspective on researching physical disability' in *Disability, Handicap & Society*, Vol 7, No 2, pp 157 - 66.

Mousley, J.A., Rice, M. & Tregenza, K. (1993) 'Integration of Students with Disabilities into Regular Schools: policy in use' in *Disability, Handicap & Society*, Vol 8, No 1, pp 59-70.

Oliver, M. (1995a) 'Defining impairment and disability: issues at stake.' Unpublished paper.

Piachaud, D. (1991) review of T. and D. Wilson (Eds) *The State and Social Welfare: the Objectives of Policy*, Longman, in *Policy Studies*, 12, 4.

Shapiro, M.J. (1988) *The Politics of Representation: Writing Practices in Biography, Photography and Policy Analysis*, Wisconsin: The University of Wisconsin Press.

Tomlinson, S. (1982) *A Sociology of Special Education*, London: Routledge & Kegan Paul.

Vlachou, A. D. (1997) *Struggles for Inclusive Education: An ethnographic study*, Buckingham: Open University Press.

Weber, M. (1964) *The Theory of Social and Economic Organization*, New York: Oxford University Press.

Policy documents

<u>UK</u>

DFEE (1997) *Excellence for All Children: Meeting Special Educational Needs*, London: HMSO (Green Paper).

<u>NSW</u>

The Integration/Inclusion Feasibility Study (1996) prepared for the Minister for Education and Training, New South Wales.

*Documents from **Kids Belong Together***, New South Wales.

(1) Epstein-Frisch, B. (1995) 'Kids Belong Together: A Campaign to Create Better Schools: Summary of Campaign Activities', typescript, 32 pp , March.

(2) Epstein-Frisch, B. (1995) (1995) 'The Inclusion Debate: What the Research Says', NSW, July, typescript, 9 pp.

(3) Kids Belong Together, 'Achieving Justice in Education', n.d., leaflet.

(4)   What has the McRae Report told us about the NSW Education System?', n.d., typescript, 3 pp.

(5) 'Action for the McCrae Report, A Coalition for the Implementation of the Integration/Inclusion Report', n.d. 1 p.

(6) 'Inclusion in Education - The Benefits', compiled by Kids Belong Together, n.d., typescript, 9 pp.

Queensland, NSW, SA, WA.

Queensland Teachers' Union (199) 'Children's rights: Are they in conflict with teacher rights?   State and Territory Round-up', P.O. Box 170, Milton BC, Queensland 4064, 20pp.

WA

Wills, D. (1996 - last update) 'Including Children Who Challenge Us Most - An A-Z of inclusionary issues: Towards an Understanding of Including Children who are most often Excluded from Typical Classrooms and Local Home Schools', Pledg Projects, 1993 - available on www and email: dicenet@dice.org.au

<u>**UNIT THREE**</u>

<u>**COMPARATIVE PERSPECTIVES ON DIFFERENCE AND
DIFFICULTY: A CROSS-CULTURAL APPROACH**</u>

<u>**FELICITY ARMSTRONG**</u>

INTRODUCTION

A particular concern of this Unit is to ask the question: what does it mean
to 'do' comparative research and what contribution can it make to our
understanding of issues relating to education, difference and disability?
We shall look critically at some models of comparative research in
education and examine what we can learn from them, both about the
research process and about ways in which different societies construct
and respond to differences between people. Particular importance will be
given to understanding differences between societies in terms of their
historical development. The Unit will introduce a number of issues and
questions which will be returned to in greater depth in the final Module
of the course *Cross Cultural Issues in Special and Inclusive Education.*

Our interest in comparative research in the context of this course centres
around the ways in which societies construct, interpret and respond to
disability and difference. In many ways some of the surface, visible
differences between these responses are quite extreme. At the same time
there appear to be similarities. These differences and similarities can be
partially explained by historic, economic and cultural factors such as
whether a country has been *coloniser* or *colonised*, its level of

'development' and the ways in which concepts such as 'equality' and 'rights' are understood and interpreted. One element in this debate is the strength of our own attitudes and assumptions which fundamentally affect the way in which we see and analyse the world. It also profoundly influences the kinds of questions we ask and the selections we make from possible knowledge or information. For example, I have just referred to the concepts of 'equality' and 'rights', but to what extent is it meaningful to use terms such as these as if they were universal, as if they would be used and understood in all societies and contexts in the same way? This is clearly not the case. Cultures do not all share common values and concerns and, to make things even more complicated, different communities within the same country may themselves hold values which are fundamentally opposed. It is important to see beyond our own context and to try and set aside what we 'know' in order that we can learn from our understanding of other cultures. This is one of the most important and difficult demands made on cross-cultural enquiry.

Until recently a number of models of comparative research have dominated the field which, it could be argued, either deny the multi-layered complexities of social relationships or are not 'comparative' at all. In the following section we will look at three of these models and briefly consider what we can learn from them.

RESEARCH AND THE ACT OF COMPARING
Although there is a large body of literature about education systems in different countries there is not a great deal on 'special education' and, until very recently, very little on what is meant by the act of making comparisons between different educational systems. Many studies which are called 'comparative' don't actually make any comparisons at all, they

merely *invite* the reader to do so by presenting a study of an education system in a particular country or of some aspect of that system. Other studies set out to make comparisons between characteristics of educational systems in different countries. Lastly, there is the 'comparative study' on a grand scale in which organisations carry out studies and present reports which try and compare education systems between two or more countries.

The varied approaches adopted by different researchers to the study of particular countries reflect fundamental differences in the way they understand the nature and purpose of research and the meanings they attach to the social relations and values which underpin the particular systems they are studying.

Research, then, is a social practice which is embedded in particular social and cultural contexts within which certain assumptions and 'ways of seeing' are powerful agents in determining research agendas, methodologies and analytical frameworks. This does not mean that researchers are conditioned in some deterministic way by the social worlds they inhabit. On the contrary, research is itself an arena for struggle between values and ideologies which are fundamentally different. As Robin Usher (1996) argues,

> '...if research is a social practice, a practice of producing certain types of knowledge that are socially validated, then as such it is a set of activities that constructs a world to be researched. When we delineate what we intend to study, when we adopt a particular theoretical position, when we ask certain questions rather than others, when we analyse and make sense of findings in one way rather

than another, when we present our findings in a particular kind of text: all this is part of constructing a researchable world. In other words, research is not simply a matter of representing, reflecting or reporting the world but of 'creating' it through representation.'

(pp 34 - 35)

The implications of these arguments in relation to cross-cultural research are manifold and the consequent difficulties facing would-be 'comparative' researchers are well documented (Meijer *et al*, 1994, Pijl *et al*, 1997).

In their book 'From Them To Us: An International Study of Inclusion in Education', Tony Booth and Mel Ainscow (1998) refer to two common 'pitfalls' of comparative research in relation to research in the area of inclusion and exclusion in education:

'...the idea that there is a single national perspective on inclusion or exclusion, and the notion that practice can be generalised across countries without attention to different contexts and meanings.

'Yet some writers present reports of their own or other countries as if they were monocultures (e.g. Mazurek and Winzer 1994; Mittler *et al* 1993). What is called a national perspective is often an official view. In the case of the UK this can be particularly problematic, given the divergence of the education systems and their basis in legislation of Scotland, Northern Ireland and England and Wales...

The tendency to present single national perspectives is often matched by a failure to describe the way practice is to be understood in its local and national context ...This lack is part of a positivist view of social science in which research in one country can be amalgamated and summed with that of another...The problem is compounded by differences of meaning of concepts, which is of particular significance in relation to categories of inability and disability. Yet, for example, in the special issues of the *European Journal of Special Needs Education* the review of European research on 'integration' is conducted as if all countries share the use of a category system used in England and Wales (Evans 1993).

(Booth and Ainscow 1998, pp 4-5)

We shall return to this question of categorisation shortly.

First, we shall consider three common models of what is frequently called 'comparative research'.

SINGLE COUNTRY STUDIES

Single country studies concentrate on one particular country. This might sound very straightforward but, in fact, case studies of individual countries are enormously varied both in form, content and purpose and these variations reflect the kind of questions and research agenda adopted by the researcher, and their particular purpose and interest in carrying out such a study. Case studies can be presented as disembodied, 'neutral' descriptive accounts, with the data selected, packaged and analysed in ways which may be driven more by the need to find, for example, common characteristics in different countries so that they can be 'compared'. Alternatively, the historic, socio-economic and cultural context of the country may be foregrounded so that differences between countries - and the values and social processes at work within them - can be better understood.

The particular interest of single country studies is that it is possible to provide a more detailed discussion of historical and cultural background than in other approaches. The researcher is free from the constraints of trying to make meaningful comparisons with other countries and hence having to select aspects which might *conceivably* be comparable, such as 'levels of integration', or categories of impairment or difference.

In fact, the first concern of single country case studies is not a comparative one. The material may be used comparatively but, like case studies in general, the main purpose is to present material which gives an in-depth portrait and analysis of a particular 'case'.

Studies of single countries can include anything from a purely descriptive account of the education system in a particular country, to a study which seeks to analyse and problematise the structures, processes and discourses of educational provision and critically examine the implications of this analysis.

ACTIVITY ONE

1. Read: Linda Ware (1998) 'USA:I Kind Of Wonder If we're Fooling Ourselves' in Booth, T and Ainscow, M. (1998) From Them To Us: An International Study of Inclusion in Education, London, Routledge. This article is in your folder of readings.

2. What questions does Linda Ware raise concerning inclusive education in the US? Could you ask similar questions concerning your own national context or are there different questions you would want to raise?

SMALL SCALE STUDIES

Some small scale studies focus on particular aspects or features of educational systems in different areas or countries. This allows the researcher to look in some detail at those aspects without having to take on whole systems. For example, a BERA (British Educational Research Association) Task Group carried out a comparative study of assessment in the educational systems of England and Wales, Scotland and Northern Ireland. In this comparative study '..the Task Group identified the key differences between these three educational systems and sought to understand the reasons why assessment policies had developed more or less differently in the systems in question.' (Broadfoot, P., Dockrell, B., Gipps, C., Harlen, W. and Nuttall, D. 1992. Included in your folder of readings). In this research, very clear objectives were identified. The purpose was '..to gain new insights concerning assessment policy' and it attempted '..to explore the likely effects of current policies and to suggest alternative approaches to meet the same purposes which would avoid some of the negative effects predicted by this analysis'.(op.cit.)

Another example of a study which looks at features or aspects of systems is a longitudinal study carried out over a period of ten years on the nature and quality of teachers' working lives in England and the USSR. These countries were chosen as 'extreme examples in the European context of, in the case of the one, the centralisation, and in the case of the other, the decentralisation of educational administration.' (Poppleton, P., Gershunsky, Boris S., Pullin, R. 1994. Included in the folder of readings).

A third example of this more focused approach is the comparative study of primary school teachers in England and France which examined differences in classroom practice (Osborn, M. and Broadfoot, P. (1992) 'A Lesson in Progress? Primary Classrooms Observed in England and France'. Included in the folder of readings).

In these examples, researchers hypothesised and reflected on differences which they found between countries or regions, without claiming that they were in a position to take all aspects of a situation into account. Nevertheless, studies which are not contextualized within the particular social and cultural framework in which they take place, will inevitably be over-simplifications and will not be able to demonstrate and provide informed insights into the structures and processes involved. The task of placing studies in their social-historical and political backgrounds raises some difficult challenges for the researcher in making commentaries and drawing out conclusions which have any meaning, and explains why comparative researchers are often rather tentative in the claims they make.

ACTIVITY TWO: READING, UNDERSTANDING AND NOTE-TAKING
Choose one of the articles mentioned above in this section (Broadfoot, et.al (1992), Poppleton, et. al, (1994), Osborn et. al, (1992). Skim-read it and make rough notes as you go along on the following questions:

1. What was the main focus (or 'research question') of the study?

2. What 'methodology' was used?

3. Summarise the research findings.

4. What evidence can you find in the article that the researchers recognise the importance of context in planning, carrying out and analysing and interpreting their research?

LARGE SCALE STUDIES

Studies which attempt to make cross-national studies of whole systems pose particular problems. An example of this is the OECD study 'Integrating Students With Special Needs Into Mainstream Schools' (OECD, 1995). In this study a number of features have been compared, such as the numbers of the school populations of different countries classified as disabled, the categories of disability in individual countries, the percentage of the school population receiving some form of special education, etc. This study provides some interesting material which demands critical examination, but it is of particular interest because of the difficulties it throws up relating to large scale comparative studies. This study offers us very little background information to help us understand the context in which particular structures and practices have been adopted. There is a considerable amount of information given about the *surface structure* of the different educational systems such as classification of disability, legislation and formal policy statements, but this does not tell us anything about the nature and complexity of the populations concerned.

When the figures are given for the school age population in special education in France, for example, important differences such as cultural and economic background are hidden. As far as the material presented in the study is concerned, the population is homogeneous. There is no possibility of exploring issues such as the over-representation of young French-north Africans in the special classes for students who experience learning difficulties in secondary education (Dumay, J-M. 1994); the effects of poverty and unemployment; the exclusion of many special institutions from the education system altogether.

A further problem which may arise in large scale studies relates to the question of data. Usually data is provided by the individual countries concerned and it is not possible to ensure uniformity in the methods used to collect or analyse data or that the data collected is of the same kind. For example, different uses of terms such as 'integration' or 'learning difficulties' may mean that different kinds of data are collected which are not comparable. Meanings can be changed or lost in the process of translation from one language to another. In the OECD study (1995) 'Integrating students with special needs into mainstream schools', data was collected on the school age population recorded as having a particular named disability. There are some very noticeable differences between countries both in the categories adopted, the number of different categories and in the numbers of children and young people identified as belonging to them.

ACTIVITY THREE

Spend a few minutes looking at Table 1 (below) which is taken from the OECD report (1995) 'Integrating students with special needs into mainstream schools'. What questions does it raise about the research methodology and processes? What issues emerge about the identification and labelling of children and young people as having particular difficulties and disabilities?

DISCUSSION

There are clearly some anomalies in the data arising from a number of sources which, in most cases, can only be guessed at. For example, there is no uniformity in the way impairments are categorised across the countries concerned so it is difficult to make comparisons. Some

TABLE 1

Terms used to describe children with special educational needs in participating countries

	1	2	3	4	5	6	7	8	9	10	11	12	13	14	15	16
Australia			*		*	→	*	→	*	*						*
Austria		*	*	*	*	*	*	*	*	*		*		*		
Belgium	*	*	*	*	*	→	*	→	*	*		*				
Canada (New Brunswick)					*	→	*	→								*
Denmark	*	*	*	*	*	→		*	*	*	*					
Finland	*	*	*	*	*	→	*	→	*	*		*			*	*
France	*	*	*		*	*	*	*	*	*					*	
Germany	*	*	*	*	*	*	*	*	*	*		*				
Greece	*	*	*	*	*	→	*	→	*	*						
Iceland	*	*	*	*		*		*	*	*	*				*	
Ireland	*	*	*	*	*	→	*	→	*	*			*		*	
Italy																*
Japan		*	*	*	*	*	*	*	*	*		*			*	
Netherlands	*	*	*	*	*	*	*	*	*	*		*			*	
Norway	*	*		*	*	→	*	*	*	*						*
Spain	*	*	*		*	→	*	→	*	*	*					*
Sweden		*			*	→	*	→		*						
Switzerland	*	*	*	*	*	*	*	*	*	*	*	*		*	*	
Turkey		*	*	*	*	→	*	→	*	*		*				*
United Kingdom																*
United States	*	*	*	*	*	→	*	→	*	*		*			*	

---

1. Mild learning difficulties, learning disabilities, specific learning disabilities, subject-related disabilities.
2. Moderate learning difficulties, educable mentally retarded, educable mental handicap, general learning disabilities, moderate mental retardation.
3. Severe learning difficulties, severe mental retardation, severe mental handicap, trainable mental handicap, profound mental handicap.
4. Speech difficulties, language and communication disabilities, specific language impairment, speech and communication difficulty, speech handicap.
5. Hearing impairment, hard of hearing.
6. Deaf.
7. Visual impairment, visual handicap, partially sighted.
8. Blind.
9. Emotional/behavioural difficulties, psycho-social disabilities, psychiatric difficulties, personality difficulties, deviant behaviour, serious emotional disturbance.
10. Physically handicapped, motor impairment, sensori-motor disabilities, orthopaedically handicapped, orthopaedic impairment.
11. Autistic
12. Chronic conditions requiring prolonged hospitalisation, paediological institutes, other health impairments.
13. Children of the travelling community.
14. Pupils whose first language is foreign.
15. Multiply-handicapped, severe sensory/mentally retarded, multiple disabilities.
16. Exceptional children, children with special educational needs, handicapped children, gifted, deaf-blindness, others.
→ These countries use one term to describe blind/partially sighted and deaf/partially hearing children.

(OECD, 1995)

countries have long lists of terms used to describe 'children with special educational needs', others present only one category, 'Special educational needs'. And what explanation can be found for the fact that in some countries, for example, there are no young people with 'speech and language difficulties?' Does this mean that there are none in some countries or that they are categorised differently or not at all? And how can we account for the fact that in the UK there are apparently *no* categories, only 'special educational needs'? In fact, we know that in the UK categorisation is alive and well. How else do pupils in the UK find themselves in different named settings ('autistic unit', 'speech and language resource centre', 'EBD school', etc.) according to the way in which their difficulties have been assessed and labelled? We should, then, look with some suspicion at data of this kind and analyse it critically.

Underlying the difficulties relating to categorisation and terminology noted above, is an issue of far greater importance than those concerned with the 'technical' problem of making comparisons between countries. This is to do with the confusion surrounding the meanings attached to the term 'disability' and its frequent use to mean 'impairment'. Thus is the OECD study (op. cit) a plethora of terms, derived from the material provided by the different countries involved in the study, is used to describe 'impairments' and 'difficulties' of all sorts, usually based on the medical 'within child' model similar to that adopted by the WHO (World Health Organisation). The authors of the report recognise this (Evans, et al 1995 pp 33 - 36) and discuss briefly what they perceive as a move away from the medical model in some countries in favour of the term *special educational needs,*

'.....following the recognition that medically based categories are not adequate in determining the educational placement of children....

'These two descriptive systems have wide ramifications both in theory and practice. Because of its derivation from a medical approach that emphasises "treatment", the categorical model implies that the learning problems lie within the individual child. On the other hand, the description of SEN recognises that educational outcome is dependent on the interaction between the child, the education provided in the school, and the influences of the home and the community more generally...' (Evans et al, 1995 p 34).

But, not only does such an analysis cling on to old assumptions which place difficulties 'within the child' through a discourse of *'having* SEN', but it fails to recognise that *disability is not an 'individual pathology' but a form of oppression and exclusion which is constructed by and within particular social and political conditions and relationships.* Different societies construct disability in culturally specific ways, expressing their particular dominant social norms and practices. This analysis reveals the *subjectivity* of the categories and labels assigned to different groups in society and offers some insights into the reasons for the wide variations between countries in the ways they recognise and identify differences between people.

CATEGORISATION AND SEGREGATION

One theme which emerges in all Units is that of categorisation and the way in which different processes of selection exclude or include certain groups.

The question of categorisation is a complex one. The ways in which groups have become identified and defined by societies are rooted in the particular historical development of those countries. In France and the UK, for example, schools were set up for the deaf and blind by religious organisations from the eighteenth century onwards. Provision for disabled children and those perceived as having learning difficulties (variously described as 'mental handicap', 'retardation' etc.) grew up in the early part of the twentieth century and the period after the second world war, particularly between the early 1950's and late 1960's, when there was a rapid proliferation of institutions for disabled children outside the education system (Armstrong, F.J. 1995). In England it was not until the 1970's that the education of all children became the responsibility of the Department of Education and Science, although how the notion of the 'education of all children' was understood and interpreted varied greatly between different Local Education Authorities across the country. In France many children still remain outside the education system and receive 'treatment', therapy and some teaching in a variety of institutions. (see Table 2 which is taken from the OECD Report (1995), 'Integrating students with special needs into mainstream schools'). Education systems and practices in other countries have developed along other, diverse routes and there are corresponding differences in the way in which different groups are categorised (see Table 3, taken from the OECD Report).

There is a common assumption underpinning western education systems that the needs of disabled children and those with difficulties in learning are best served when there are effective systems for the early identification of 'conditions' and difficulties with a network of corresponding educational provision to respond to them. On one level,

TABLE 2

Proportion of children with SEN for whom provision is made: in special schools and units, special classes, and outside the education system

	% of pupils with SEN for whom provision is made	Outside education	In special school and unit	In special class	Total outside mainstream
Australia	5.22	nil	0.63	0.92	1.55
Austria	2.55	< 0.1	2.55	< 0.1	2.55
Belgium	3.08	< 0.1	3.08	n.a.	3.08
Canada (New Brunswick)	10.79 [1]	nil	n.a.	n.a.	n.a.
Denmark	13.03	nil	0.65	0.98	1.63
Finland	17.08	0.14	1.85	0.83	2.82
France	3.54	1.38 [2]	1.26	0.64	3.28
Germany [3]	7.00	nil	3.69	n.a.	3.69
Greece	0.86	0.18	0.20	0.48 [4]	0.38
Iceland	15.71	nil	0.58	0.71 [4]	1.29
Ireland	1.45	0.22	1.04	0.41	1.67
Italy	1.27	n.a.	n.a.	n.a.	n.a.
Japan [5]	0.89	nil	0.37	0.52	0.89
Netherlands	3.63	< 0.1	3.63	nil	3.63
Norway [6]	6.00	< 0.1	0.6		< 0.7
			(schools and classes)		
Spain	2.03	n.a.	0.80	0.23	1.03
Sweden	1.60	nil	1.03	→	1.03
Switzerland	4.90	nil	4.90		4.90
			(schools and classes)		
Turkey [7]	0.74	n.a.	0.28	0.33	0.61
United Kingdom [8]	1.85	nil	1.3	n.a.	1.3
United States	7.00	nil	n.a.	n.a.	2.90 [9]

n.a. = not available.

1. This figure includes gifted students.
2. Children in establishments provided by the Ministry of Social Security. A proportion of these are educated in ordinary schools.
3. Former Federal Republic of Germany only (1989). The 7% figure is an estimate.
4. Part-time only; otherwise, in ordinary class.
5. Column one covers those children of compulsory school age.
6. Many more than the 6% quoted have individualised help for minor disabilities.
7. An estimated 14% of children between 0 and 18 years are handicapped.
8. England and Wales only.
9. This figure was derived by adding together children who were receiving a good to fair proportion of their education outside the mainstream as described in the detailed notes on the United States.

(OECD, 1995)

TABLE 3

Percentage of total school population classified as handicapped and classification of various handicaps as percentage of the SEN population in 21 OECD countries

	% SEN	1	2	3	4	5	6	7	8	9	10	11	12	13	14	15	16 Others
Australia[1]	5.22					10.89	↑	2.92	↑	2.80	2.50		4.60				
Austria	2.55	40.95	66.30	16.70	3.20	0.80	2.10	0.70	0.30	9.30	5.00					2.41	
Belgium[2]	3.08		28.42	6.28	4.15	2.40	↑	1.20	↑								
Canada (New Brunswick)	10.79					0.27		0.18									
Denmark	13.02																
Finland	17.08	43.49	8.36	2.43	26.39	0.89	↑	0.19	↑	12.34	1.21						4.68
France	3.54	32.03	11.57	3.60		4.02	1.10	1.39	0.43	36.18	7.56					5.21	0.81
Germany[3,4]	7.00	55.00	15.30		8.01	1.94		0.81	0.51	3.54	5.48		3.00				
Greece	0.86	55.62	15.31	10.84		4.60	0.23	0.69	↑		2.74						10.20
Iceland[4]	15.71	46.40	1.65	1.00	0.16					0.49	0.23						96.29
Ireland	1.45		18.82	1.64		5.97	↑	1.23	↑	6.14	4.09	0.12		13.91		0.39	
Italy	1.27																
Japan	0.89		41.72	23.57	4.64	1.13	3.19	0.15	1.30	8.58	10.58		5.13				
Netherlands	3.63	41.19	31.69	6.98	0.32	3.80	0.81	0.28	0.21	5.23	3.20		4.72			1.58	
Norway[5]	6.00	56.00	↑	↑	5.00	3.00	↑	2.00	↑	24.00	5.00						5.00
Spain[6]	2.03	35.80	12.00	8.10		5.71	3.11	1.43	↑	7.49	7.44	1.28					20.70
Sweden	1.60	68.56		↑		9.34		6.22	0.31		12.45						
Switzerland	4.90	52.30	20.20		2.40	2.10	↑	0.60	↑	14.20	1.90		0.30		5.10		0.89
Turkey[7]	0.74		54.78	3.12		37.65	↑	5.60	↑		1.25						
United Kingdom	1.85																
United States	7.00	49.11	12.66	↑	22.68	1.36	↑	0.54	↑	8.99	1.13		1.27			2.24	0.0

Columns:

1. Mild learning difficulties, learning disabilities, specific learning disabilities, subject-related disabilities.
2. Moderate learning difficulties, educable mentally retarded, educable mental handicap, general learning disabilities, moderate mental retardation.
3. Severe learning difficulties, severe mental retardation, severe mental handicap, trainable mental handicap, profound mental handicap.
4. Speech difficulties, language and communication disabilities, specific language impairment, speech and communication difficulty, speech handicap.
5. Hearing impairment, hard of hearing.
6. Deaf.
7. Visual impairment, visual handicap, partially sighted.
8. Blind.
9. Emotional/behavioural difficulties, psycho-social disabilities, psychiatric difficulties, personality difficulties, deviant behaviour, serious emotional disturbance.
10. Physically handicapped, motor impairment, sensori-motor disabilities, orthopaedically handicapped, orthopaedic impairment.
11. Autistic.
12. Chronic conditions requiring prolonged hospitalisation, paediological institutes, other health impairments.
13. Children of the travelling community.
14. Pupils whose first language is foreign.
15. Multiply-handicapped, severe sensory/mentally retarded, multiple disabilities.
16. Exceptional children, children with special educational needs, handicapped children, gifted, deaf-blindness, others.

Notes:

1. See section on Australia in appendices for further explanation.
2. Some column entries are derived from several figures provided by Belgium.
3. Former Federal Republic of Germany only (1989).
4. Figures for individual disabilities are only for children in segregated special education.
5. Many more than the 6% quoted have individualised help for minor disabilities.
6. Breakdown of columns 1, 2 and 3 given by countries' representatives since only one category is used in Spain to cover the three utilised here.
7. Special schools only.
↑ These countries use one term to describe mentally retarded, blind/partially sighted and deaf/partially hearing children.

(OECD, 1995)

there is a belief that the more provision there is to meet a diversity of needs, the better things are. But there are a number of questions we should ask. First of all, how are needs defined and by whom? Not, surely, by disabled people themselves, but by the professionals who make decisions and advise parents on their behalf. Secondly, if special educational provision is offered according to the identification of a primary impairment, then doesn't the difficulty or impairment become the defining feature of the child? Doesn't the individual child as person become lost behind the label, limiting expectations and opportunities and creating a social otherness and difference to which different forms of inclusion and exclusion are inextricably bound? Such practices, enshrined in the statementing procedures in England in Wales, are disabling.

As we have seen, countries categorise disabilities in different ways and this must be one explanation for the large differences which exist between countries in the percentage of the school age population reported 'with identified special needs'. In Table 4 (taken from the OECD report 'Integrating students with special needs into mainstream schools') the numbers of pupils identified as having special needs varies between 0.74 (Turkey) and 17.08 (Finland). It would be interesting to look for explanations of these differences. At first sight, we might hypothesise that the percentage of pupils identified as having special educational needs would be greater in proportion to the number of 'categories of handicap' recognised by different countries. In addition, perhaps economic factors are a consideration. Is there a relationship between economic wealth of a country and the numbers of pupils identified as having special educational needs? After all, Turkey has only 5 official categories and Greece, also with a low percentage of pupils identified as

TABLE 4

Pupils with identified special educational needs as percentages of the total school population in 21 OECD countries

	% SEN	1	2	3	4	5	6	7	8	9	10	11	12	13	14	15	16 Others
Australia[1]	5.22						↑	0.15	↑								
Austria	2.55		1.66	0.42	0.08	0.57	↑	0.02	0.01	0.07	0.06		0.16				
Belgium[2]	3.08	1.26	0.88	0.19	0.13	0.02	0.05	0.04	↑	0.29	0.16		0.07				
Canada (New Brunswick)	10.79					0.08		0.18									
Denmark	13.03					0.27											
Finland	17.08		1.43	0.42	4.51	0.15	↑	0.03	↑	2.11	0.21						0.79
France	3.54		0.41	0.13		0.14	↑	0.05	0.01	1.29	0.27					0.08	0.03
Germany[3,4]	7.00	2.04	0.56	↑	0.30	0.07	0.04	0.03	0.02	0.13	0.20		0.11			0.19	
Greece	0.86	0.48	0.13	0.09		0.04	0.04	0.01	n.a.								0.09
Iceland[4]	15.71		0.26	0.16		0.09	↑	0.02	↑	0.08	0.04	0.02		0.20		0.006	15.13
Ireland	1.45		0.27	0.02	0.002	0.09	↑	0.02	↑	0.08	0.05						
Italy	1.27																
Japan	0.89		0.37	0.21	0.04	0.01	0.03	0.001	0.01	0.08	0.09		0.05				
Netherlands	3.63	1.50	1.15	0.25	0.01	0.14	0.03	0.01	0.008	0.19	0.12		0.17			0.06	
Norway[5]	6.00		<				NOT AVAILABLE										>
Spain[6]	2.03	0.73	0.24	0.16		0.12	0.05	0.03	0.005	0.15	0.15	0.03					0.42
Sweden	1.60		1.1	↑		0.15		0.10			0.20					0.001	
Switzerland	4.90	2.56	0.99	↑	0.12	0.10	↑	0.03	↑	0.70	0.09		0.02		0.25		0.04
Turkey[7]	0.74		0.32	0.02		0.22	↑	0.03	↑		0.007						
United Kingdom	1.85																
United States	7.00	3.17	0.82	↑	1.46	0.09	↑	0.03	↑	0.58	0.07		0.08			0.14	0.002

Columns:

1. Mild learning difficulties, learning disabilities, specific learning disabilities, subject-related disabilities.
2. Moderate learning difficulties, educable mentally retarded, educable mental handicap, general learning disabilities, moderate mental retardation.
3. Severe learning difficulties, severe mental retardation, severe mental handicap, trainable mental handicap, profound mental handicap.
4. Speech difficulties, language and communication disabilities, specific language impairment, speech and communication difficulty, speech handicap.
5. Hearing impairment, hard of hearing.
6. Deaf.
7. Visual impairment, visual handicap, partially sighted.
8. Blind.
9. Emotional/behavioural difficulties, psycho-social difficulties, psychiatric difficulties, personality difficulties, deviant behaviour, serious emotional disturbance.
10. Physically handicapped, motor impairment, sensori-motor disabilities, orthopaedically handicapped, orthopaedic impairment.
11. Autistic.
12. Chronic conditions requiring prolonged hospitalisation, paediological institutes, other health impairments.
13. Children of the traveling community.
14. Pupils whose first language is foreign.
15. Multiply-handicapped, severe sensory/mentally retarded, multiple disabilities.
16. Exceptional children, children with special educational needs, handicapped children, gifted, deaf-blindness, others.

Notes:

n.a. = not available.

1. See section on Australia in appendices for further explanation.
2. Some column entries are derived from several figures provided by Belgium.
3. Former Federal Republic of Germany only (1989).
4. Figures for individual disabilities are only or children in segregated special education.
5. Many more than the 6% quoted have individualised help for minor disabilities.
6. Breakdown of columns 1, 2 and 3 given by countries' representatives since only one category is used in Spain to cover the three utilised here.
7. Special schools only.
↑ These countries use one term to describe mentally retarded, blind/partially sighted and deaf/partially hearing children.

(OECD, 1995)

having special educational needs (0.86), has only 6 categories. But how do we explain the figures for Japan where 0.89% of the school population is identified as having special educational needs but there are 10 official categories of disability listed? And what about Italy, Denmark and the UK? These countries don't appear to acknowledge any official categorisation according to disability of pupils.

All these questions raise important issues concerning the nature and complexity of 'comparative' research. They also raise other questions about the ways in which different societies construct disability and difference, and the ways these constructions become institutionalised through practice.

How can we explain, for example, the *practice* of identifying and categorising disabilities and learning difficulties in the UK?. The term 'special educational needs' was introduced following the Warnock report and the 1981 Education Act to replace the eleven 'categories of disability which were previously used'. The **stated** *policy* behind this move was that we should look at children's individual needs, not the label they carried, and that these should be met as far as possible in ordinary schools. In *practice*, however, the policy has been to assess pupils and categorise them through the process of the multi-professional assessment which is used to allocate pupils to particular educational settings and allocate resources. In general, allocation to provision is resource lead and much will depend on the kind of provision available in particular authorities. In an area in which there are Units for pupils with speech and language difficulties, children whose difficulties are related to communication problems are more likely to attend a language unit than a special school for children with learning difficulties. Decisions which are made concerning the closing down of special schools or the opening up of specialist units, decisions which are taken concerning integration, in-service courses for teachers, the use of funds allocated to Local Authorities by central Government for the alteration of school buildings to make them more accessible, all these decisions and choices have been mediated by policies made at local level. These policies will often be made by schools and their governing bodies and will reflect the different values and cultures of particularly schools.

Gillian Fulcher has argued that policy *is* practice. This counters the assumption that policies are made by governments and these policies are put into practice 'at the coal face'. Policy, she argues, is made at all levels and in all arenas (Fulcher, G. 1989). This view of 'policy' as being acted out at all levels of the system, explains to some extent why - in spite of central government having 'abolished categories of handicap' - the practice of sifting, sorting and labelling pupils is a deeply rooted part of the educational environment. It also explains why there are such large differences in the numbers of pupils in segregated schools and units in different parts of the country (Norwich, B. 1994).

Somehow, 'labels' and the processes of assessment and selection which surround them, are very powerful. These labels may be attached to institutions and are transferred to pupils when they pass through their gates. Or they may be attached to pupils in the formal and informal process of assessment and used to sort them into separate groups. In either case, categorisation works against the inclusion of pupils with disabilities and learning difficulties in ordinary schools. The assigning of categories and their labels to certain groups in society is a powerful part of the drawing up and maintenance of boundaries between what is 'normal' and accepted, and what is 'abnormal' or deviant and deserving of different treatment or exclusion. There is overwhelming evidence of the negative, stereotypical and discriminatory role played by practices of labelling in different societies, and this has been the subject of considerable debate and theorising, (For an overview and discussion of this debate, read pp 38 - 55 in 'Struggles for Inclusive Education' (Vlachou, 1997).

It is difficult to conceive of a situation in which we could get rid of labels and categories as long as specialist settings exist. On the other hand, as long as ordinary schools fail to provide an education for all, which means an acceptance and celebration of difference, then segregated schools and units will survive along with their labels.

There are two further questions we need to ask. How can we talk about the kinds of curricula and organisation schools need to develop if they are to become truly inclusive without using labels? And how can the knowledge and experience of specialists be drawn upon and used in the process of building school communities for all?

Although the studies discussed in this section here are not 'comparative', a number of common themes do emerge which invite comparison. These are not necessarily associated with statistical data or legislation (although these may give us useful insights into broader issues). They are more concerned with issues relating to historical development, the ways in which different societies understand and construct difference, the social and economic context and rationales for particular events and paths taken.

CONTEXT, CULTURE AND THE CONSTRUCTION OF DIFFERENCE

> **ACTIVITY FOUR**
> **Key Reading**
> Read: Miles. M. (1992) 'Concepts of mental retardation in Pakistan: toward cross-cultural and historical perspectives', <u>Disability, Handicap and Society</u> Vol. 7, No. 3, 1992
>
> Make some rough notes as you go along. When you have finished reading the article, pull out one argument put forward by Miles which you think is particularly important.
> Write some notes on it, adding your own reflections and comments. You should try to link what you write to other ideas or articles which you have read.

DISCUSSION

Here are some notes (tidied up and re-worked for the purposes of presentation in this Module!) which I made after reading this article. You may well have identified other points of interest for discussion.

> *This article raises questions concerning the social construction of difference across cultures which have important implications for the researcher. It contests assumptions that concepts - and the values attached to them - such as 'independence' and 'dependency' have a universal, omnipotent meaning and acceptance. It also challenges western assumptions about the relationship between economic and cultural 'development' and human rights (and these concepts must be seen too as social constructs). According to Miles (1992) Muslims '..debated the civil rights of mentally retarded persons a thousand years before the current Western debate.'(Miles, 1992).*

Miles' account also reveals some of the factors and processes involved in the social construction of learning difficulties within groups in different societies.

"Mental' retardation' understood thus, is socially and individually noticed, constructed and felt. If one of the educated élite has a teenage child who has not learnt to read even after tutoring, and who cannot be trusted to serve tea and make polite conversation with parental guests, the child may be deemed to have mental retardation...However, the criterion of 'failure to learn to read' would hardly indicate mental retardation in the general population, where less than 30% of adults have learnt to read...'Unreliable in polite talk and in serving tea respectfully to guests' would equally be misleading as a criterion of mental retardation if applied to English adolescents.' (Miles, 1992 p 236).

This article draws attention to the importance not just of place and culture, but of class, caste and gender too in constructing learning difficulties. It also shows how misleading it is to make sweeping generalisation about how families respond to children's disabilities and learning difficulties in a particular country. There are also questions raised about the generalisability of 'models' such as the social model and the medical model. How does the view of some families in many cultures that their child's impairment is possessed by a spirit fit in with the dominant discourses in western academic writing on this subject?

These questions give us much food for thought. Not least, about the complexities involved in making comparisons between societies. The temptation is to try and map on the 'data' we accumulate and the observations we make about other societies to our own familiar tried and tested ways of thinking. This doesn't work. For this reason, I prefer a 'cross-cultural' approach to a comparative one. Cross-cultural enquiry allows us to look at social change in historical, cultural and political frameworks across different societies, without the altering constraint of imposing technical ways of comparing them.

EXCLUSION AND INCLUSION IN SOCIAL CONTEXTS

The concept of exclusion should be understood in local contexts. For example, many economically poorer countries do not have the resources to provide an education system for all children and young people. When resources are scarce, many children are excluded or filtered out progressively from the school system from an early age. Processes of selection and exclusion take place in economically wealthier countries but at a later stage in the education process. A system of examinations at different stages along the route towards further and higher education is used to assess and exclude people thus legitimating an increasingly selective process (Bourdieu and Passeron, 1977). In England and Wales, for example, the introduction of a national curriculum and standardised testing have lead to greater selection and exclusion practices at increasingly earlier stages in the educational process (Johnson, R. 1991a, Harris, S. 1994, Armstrong, F. 1999).

The point is, all societies exclude some groups of people from ordinary education; the origins and forms of these exclusions are diverse and are only partially linked to economic development. As important are the attitudes towards difference in any given society. Practices which include or exclude on the basis of disability or perceived ability are only part of a wider system which include or exclude people at different structural and cultural levels in society.

We reject the medical model of disability which presents disabilities and learning difficulties as arising from deficits within the person. However, we recognise that disabilities may arise out of social and curricula responses to impairments such as sensory or physical difficulties. These, in their turn, may arise out of the social and economic conditions in society which fail to provide adequate food, shelter and medical care. The right to an adequate quality of life should be a basic human right. This is an issue for the so-called 'advanced' countries where many people do not have this right, as well as in poorer parts of the world. But Inigo Cavanagh (1994) has demonstrated the inequalities which exist between high and low income countries as well as some relationships between low income and disability in poorer countries. You will find his article 'Disability and special educational provision for children with disabilities in low income countries' in your folder of readings.

WORLD POPULATIONS

There is a tendency to talk about nationalities and populations as if they were homogeneous groups sharing particular histories and characteristics. This is misleading. The populations of the world are constantly shifting and changing. This has always been true but the twentieth century has seen a massive acceleration in this process as a result of wars between nations, civil wars, struggles for independence, famine and disease, natural disasters and the development of new technologies in communication and transport . The social and educational consequences of such movements have received little attention in much of the literature on education, but they are dramatically present in most inner-city classrooms and in different forms in communities all over the world.

Difficulties in learning (often conceptualised as 'special needs') may arise as a result of cultural, social and linguistic disruption to young people who have to move to different countries or areas. Others may experience oppression because their language and culture is not recognised or is devalued by the dominant culture of the country in which they live. Young refugees may experience deep trauma and 'cultural violation' in the countries they seek refuge in and will often experience difficulties in learning. Populations such as the Maoris in New Zealand or black Africans in S. Africa are particularly vulnerable educationally in countries which have been colonised by other groups. The difficulties some experience in learning may not be associated with a disability, but are created through the failure of educational structures and practices to respond to difference in ways which recognise all children and young people as equal. This failure is present both at an organisational level and at the level of the curriculum.

SPECIAL EDUCATION AND THE POST-COLONIAL CONTEXT

There are few countries which can claim not to have been affected by the past or recent history of colonialism in some form or other, and education systems are an area of the infra structure of any society which is particularly sensitive to the impact of social, cultural and political change.

Colonialism has, in effect, turned round on itself and - years after 'independence' has apparently been achieved in Africa, Asia and the Caribbean - is continuing to work through forms of domination and oppression in European social arenas themselves. We can see this being acted out through the values and content of school curricula in different countries and the lack of place given to the culture and knowledge of different communities within those curricula.

In many countries which have been colonised, the education system imposed by the old colonising 'motherland' often lives on. The space it occupies is pervasive at many levels of the education system, not least at the level of a colonising cultural interference. Edward Said (1994) has written of the importance of the colonial experience as handed down as 'culture' in newly independent states:

> '...the cultural horizons of nationalism may be fatally limited by the common history it presumes of coloniser and colonised. Imperialism after all was a co-operative venture, and a salient trait of its modern form is that it was (or claimed to be) an educational movement; it set out quite consciously to modernise, develop, instruct, and civilise. The annals of schools, missions, universities, scholarly societies, hospitals in Asia, Africa, Latin America, Europe, and America are filled with this history, which over time established so-called modernising trends as much as it muted the harsher aspects of imperial domination. But at its centre it preserved the nineteenth century divide between native and Westerner.

> The great colonial schools, for example, taught generations of the native bourgeoisie important truths about history, science, culture. Out of that learning process millions grasped the fundamentals of modern life, yet remained subordinate dependants of an authority based elsewhere than in their own lives. Since one of the purposes of colonial education was to promote the history of France or Britain, that same history also demoted the native history. Thus for the native there was always the Englands, Frances,

Germanys, Hollands as distant repositories of the Word, despite the affinities developed between native and 'white man' during the years of productive collaboration..." (pp 269 - 270).

The transplantation and imposition of educational systems from colonising to colonised countries was both a cultural and political expression of imperialism which, rather than having left its legacies behind in the contemporary world, continues to exercise an insidious and virulent role in defining and rewarding particular knowledge paradigms.

One important question to ask concerns the effect that colonial history has had upon the construction of 'norms' and the categorisation of difference in different contexts. This question will be explored in the Module *Cross-cultural issues in special and inclusive education.*

COLONIALISM, CHRISTIANITY AND EDUCATION

For the British colonies, along with the arrival of school certificate examinations and then 'O' and 'A' levels', a eurocentric curriculum, mission schools, a British monarch and Baden Powell, came 'special education' as well. True, the distribution of schools of all kinds was uneven in the colonies and in most cases were mediated by church missions and reserved for a 'deserving' few. Post-colonial countries are still, to some extent, encumbered by the attitudes and disabling categories foisted on them by their former colonisers. Western responses to disability sat comfortably with colonial discourses of difference relating to race, culture and the inculcation of Christian belief. Of course, it was not just colonised countries which were affected by Western influences and constructions, but all those countries who were the subject of an expansion of trade and the search for new markets and sources of cheap goods and labour. The Christian church also played a complementary but different role in the 'civilisation' and conversion of populations through their missions, medical and educational work. Here is a description of some of the work done by Christian missionaries in China by the Rev. A.H. Smith, published in 1907 by the Young Christians Missionary Union:

'Asylums or villages for lepers have been established in five different provinces where excellent work has been done. There are eight orphanages (one of them in Hong Kong, but conducted by missionaries to the Chinese) caring for a great number of children - mostly girls. Eleven schools or asylums for the blind - the best known being that of Mr Murray in Peking - are working what the Chinese justly regard as daily miracles, rescuing from uselessness a class hitherto quite hopeless. A school for deaf mutes in Chefoo is an object-lesson of what may be done on behalf of that large and unfortunate class. An asylum for the insane, begun under great difficulties by the late Dr. J.G.Kerr at Canton, is likewise a pioneer in caring for a numerous but hitherto neglected class. Some practical Christian philanthropy is often a more effective testimony than any preaching. As a Japanese Christian said of the work among lepers: 'It will do more for Christianity than anything that has been done. My people can argue as cleverly as your people about religion, but they know nothing of such love as this.'

In the mission-station there will usually be established at an early stage a school for boys. The first pupils are any who can be got, but at a later period they will be mainly or wholly from Christian families, studying Christian

books under a Christian teacher as well as the
Chinese classics. These rudimentary
beginnings will probably develop into a well-
graded system of instruction, ending in a
thoroughly equipped college.' (pp 203-204).

This is an interesting passage because it shows the inseparable links
between the preaching of Christian beliefs and values with the spread of
'good works' in terms of medical aid, schools for disabled children,
orphanages and the establishment of Christian schools. The missionaries
understood the importance of including some aspects of Chinese culture
in the curriculum as well as Christianity. At the same time, the mission
schools became increasingly selective, reserving places for the children
of Christian families. Educational advancement could be promoted by
becoming a Christian (and no doubt Christian advancement could be
promoted by becoming 'educated').

CONCLUSION

This Unit has raised a number of questions about the nature and
challenges of 'comparative research'. It has looked at some traditional
models of research and discussed their strengths and weaknesses. A
critique of a large-scale study in particular pointed to some of the pitfalls
and difficulties associated with this kind of research. This critique was
used to introduce a discussion of categorisation and labelling, arguing
that categories of impairment or difference are socially constructed.

In the second half of the Unit we have introduced a number of ideas and
arguments concerning the usefulness of cross-cultural research, rather
than the traditional 'comparative' approaches. The cross-cultural
paradigm is more powerful in terms of the possibilities it opens up of

trying to understand different societies, their complexities and what we can learn from them.

Some of the questions raised in this Unit are not ones which usually figure in traditional accounts of comparative research, but they are central to a cross-cultural perspective which tries to take into account both the cultural and political legacies of historical change and the underlying processes and values within different contemporary national contexts.

Of course, the Unit could only begin to introduce such issues and could not possibly examine them in any depth. They will be returned to in a number of different national contexts in Module 4, 'Cross-cultural Issues in Special and Inclusive Education'.

REFERENCES

Armstrong, F.J. (1999) 'The Curriculum as Alchemy: The Struggles for Cultural Space in School' in *Curriculum Studies*, Vol 3, No 1.

Armstrong, F.J. (1995) 'Appellation Controlée': mixing and sorting in the French Education System' in Potts, P., Armstrong, F.J., Masterton, M. (Eds) (1995) *Equality and Diversity in Education 2: National and International Contexts*, London: Routledge.

Booth, T. and Ainscow, M. (Eds) (1998) *From Them To Us: An International Study of Inclusion in Education*, London: Routledge.

Booth, T. and Ainscow, M. (1998) 'USA Response: Liberating voices?', Booth, T. and Ainscow, M.(Eds) (1998) *From Them To Us: An International Study of Inclusion in Education*, London: Routledge.

Bourdieu, P. and Passeron, J.C. (1977) *Reproduction in Education, Society and Culture*, London: Sage.

Broadfoot, P., Dockrell, B., Gipps, C., Harlen, W. & Nuttall, D. (1992) *A Comparative Study of assessment in the educational systems of England and Wales, Scotland and Northern Ireland*, British Educational Research Association.

Cavanagh, I. (1994) 'Disability and special provision for children with disabilities in low income countries.' in *European Journal of Special Needs Education*, Vol 9, No 1 (1994), pp 67 - 79.

Dumay, J.M. (1994) *L'Ecole Agressée*, Paris: Belfond.

Evans, J., Evans, P., McGovern, Mary Ann (1995) 'Statistics' in OECD (1995) *Integrating students with special needs into mainstream schools*, Paris: OECD.

Fulcher, G. (1989) *Disabling Policies*, London: Falmer Press.

Fulcher, G. (1993) 'Schools and Contests: A Reframing of the Effective Schools Debate?' in Slee, R. (Ed) (1993) *Is There a Desk With My Name On It?*, Lewes: The Falmer Press.

Harris, S. (1994), 'Entitled to What? Control and Autonomy in School: a student perspective' in *International Studies in Sociology of Education*, Vol 4, No 1, pp 57 - 76.

Johnson, R (1991a) ' A new road to serfdom? A critical history of the 1988 Act' in Cultural Studies Group, University of Birmingham (1991) *Education Limited: Schooling and Training and the New Right Since 1979*, London: Unwin Hyman.

Miles, M. (1992) 'Concepts of Mental Retardation in Pakistan: toward cross-cultural and historical perspectives' in *Disability, Handicap and Society*, Vol 7, No 3, pp 235 - 255.

Norwich, B. (1990) *Segregation and Inclusion: English LEA Statistics 1988 - 92*, Bristol: CSIE.

Mazurek, K and Winzner, M.A. (Eds) (1994) *Comparative Studies in Special Education*, Washington DC: Gallaudet University Press

Mittler, P., Brouillette, R. and Harris, D.(Eds) (1993) *World Yearbook of Education: Special Needs Education*, London: Kogan Page.

OECD (1995) *Integrating students with special needs into mainstream schools*, Paris: OECD.

Osborn, M. and Broadfoot, P. (1992) 'A Lesson in Progress? Primary Classrooms Observed in England and France' in *Oxford Review of Education*, Vol 18, No 1, 1992, pp 2 - 15.

Poppleton, P., Gershunsky, Boris, S., Pullin, P. (1994) 'Changes in Administrative Control and Teacher Satisfaction in England and the USSR' in *Comparative Education Review*, No 38, Vol 8, pp 323 - 346.

Said, E. (1994) *Culture and Imperialism*, London:Vintage.

Slee, R. (Ed) (1993) *Is There a desk With My Name on It? The Politics of Integration*, Lewes: Falmer Press.

Smith, A. (1907) *The Uplift of China*, London: Young Christians' Missionary Union.

Usher, R. (1996) 'Textuality and Reflexivity in educational research' in Scott, D. and Usher, R. (Eds) (1996) *Understanding Educational Research*, London: Routledge.

Vlachou, A. (1997) *Struggles for Inclusive Education*, Buckingham: Open University Press.

Ware, L. (1998) 'USA: I wonder if we're fooling ourselves' in Booth, T. and Ainscow, M. (Eds) *From Them To Us: An International Study of Inclusion in Education*, London: Routledge.

UNIT FOUR

INCLUSION AND EXCLUSION:

ISSUES FOR DEBATE

JENNY CORBETT

INTRODUCTION

This unit will focus on a re-examination of current insights and ideas surrounding the question of inclusion and exclusion in education. Tensions and relationships between these factors will be identified and analysed through diverse discourses and the perspectives of key participants. The two course readers, "Special Educational Needs in the Twentieth Century" (Corbett, 1998) and "Disabling Policies" (Fulcher, 1989), both reflect an interest in international perspectives, the use of language and policy development. There will be references made to them throughout the unit.

There have been many discussions on what is meant by the term "inclusion" and this has formed the substance of much argument over the semantics of inclusive ideology. Some recent debates will be evaluated in the literature review which begins this unit. It is important to reflect on the emotions surrounding so contentious an issue and to realise that inclusion is not just an intellectual argument but is a commitment to ideals. Inclusive ideology is about fundamental value systems and, as such, cannot be usefully divorced from feelings.

It is important to be aware of key legislative changes and those issues of pedagogy and student experiences as they relate to teaching and learning, a differentiated curriculum and peer support networks. These are the frameworks which can structure an inclusive system. Yet, they are insufficient of themselves. How participants and key players really feel about the inclusion or exclusion of different groups and individuals is a critical indicator of how effectively an inclusive ideology can be implemented. It is through a critical analysis of diverse discourses that these real feelings may be assessed and understood.

PERSPECTIVES ON INCLUSION

In the third reading for this unit (Rouse and Florian, 1997) there is an extensive bibliography of recent texts on issues related to inclusive education in the market place. These will form a sound basis for your background reading. They do not, however, bring you up to date with more recent books and articles or with some key developments in disability theory. In this introductory literature review, I shall discuss some current debates on issues relating to inclusion and exclusion and will indicate how you might use the two course readers.

Fulcher (1989) argues that policy is made at all levels in the educational apparatus. It is useful to start any analysis of recent literature with policy statements. Both the Special Educational Needs Code of Practice (DfEE, 1994) and the more recent Special Educational Needs Green Paper (DfEE, 1997) express a conditional commitment to inclusion, which takes account of what is considered to be appropriate for professionals and parents. Fulcher claims that terms like "appropriate" tend to distract most people's attention from the moral judgements which are being made. It also might imply that there is a universally accepted understanding of what is appropriate in teaching and learning situations rather than recognising that what is seen as natural in one setting may be unacceptable in another, according to cultural, economic and social differences (Corbett, 1998).

The Salamanca Statement (UNESCO, 1994) goes well beyond this conditional commitment to inclusion in maintaining that every child has a fundamental right to education and that children with special educational needs should have access to regular schools. Where a conceptual dilemma arises for many theorists is in addressing the gap between the ideal and the reality. Booth (1996) argues that those who present inclusion as an attainable state in which good practice can be identified risk reducing the need to see inclusion as an unending set of processes which combine increasing participation with reducing exclusion. He brings together notions of mainstream schooling, cultures and communities, rather than isolating education from its context. As recent research on the relationship between truancy and school exclusion indicates, the community may be one which promotes a feeling of social exclusion and fails to support an inclusive ideology (Social Exclusion Unit, 1998).

Slee (1998) reflects that certain forms of schooling foster increased levels of exclusion. The focus upon selection, back to basics, market competition, inspection, national standardising and league tables can lead to conservative special education theorising. The impetus to support radical educational reform can become muted when set in the context of so competitive a system. This has influenced the use of labelling such that there is no longer a stigma attached to specific labels if they can attract resources and specialist treatments. Slee (1998) refers to the label of Attention Deficit Hyperactivity Disorder (ADHD) as mainly serving the needs of other learners, teachers and parents in helping to control and remove from the mainstream those who present particular problems for behaviour management. He does not see the label as helping the individuals as such, other than marking them out as different.

Peters (1996) suggests that labelling theory, social control theory, medical sociology and the study of deviance still place disabled people as the Other in society. She looks beyond sociology to areas like feminist theory in order to liberate her consciousness. Her writing is characteristic of many disabled feminists in being deliberately personal and direct, drawing from her own feelings and life experience. As I suggested in the introduction, inclusive ideology is about emotional responses and this is one of the areas in which disability theory can inform educational debates.

In a lively and stimulating analysis, Priestley (1998) brings together some of the recent theoretical debates in disability theory showing how individual and social models, materialist and idealist theories can contribute to our wider understanding of value systems and material relationships. For those wishing to develop a deeper awareness of the complexities and contradictions inherent in any conceptual evaluation of what constitutes real inclusion in education, a side-step into disability theory is invaluable. It also sets education into the broad cultural and community values which influence and sustain it. As Fulcher says, the struggles to develop policy and to dominate discourses occur in many different arenas, including both in the wider social world and in the classroom. Expertise is not bias-free, for we need to note that,

> It is because competing priorities can be
> prevalent within the agendas of the
> professional carers in institutions, community
> services and bureaucratic systems that
> disabled people and those marginalised by
> poverty and social stigma can be confronted
> by professional stereotyping even before they
> meet with public prejudice.
>
> (Corbett, 1998, p.52)

A return to medical models of labelling, such as ADHD, autism and dyslexia, marks the individualised culture in which competition for scarce resources determines that deficits are accentuated.

In higher education this has led to an epidemic of dyslexia labelling, in order to gain the Disabled Student's Allowance (DSA) which can ensure additional tuition and technological support. Students without the labels but who require some learning support in their university studies can find themselves with minimal rights in this current market (Corbett & Parker, 1998). They need the label to get the level of support which might help them to stay the course and complete a degree rather than drop-out. Exclusion at this level is more a matter of finding it impossible to cope rather than being considered unacceptable in behaviour.

Creating an inclusive school, college or university culture is about pro-active approaches which help to counter moves towards exclusion. As Booth and Ainscow (1998) state, inclusion is an unending process connected to exclusion, which applies to all kinds of exclusion and is not limited to students with disabilities and difficulties.

In their recent analysis of theorising special education, Clark, Dyson and Millward (1998) suggest that special education needs to be reconnected into debates on fundamental educational issues. They fear that it has become trapped into a repetition of sterile arguments which prevent the growth of new ways of understanding and acting for particular times and places.

In their recent research into international approaches to inclusive practices, Booth and Ainscow (1998) illustrate that there are many different and equally effective ways in which inclusion can be supported within the curriculum, regional policy and pedagogy. If an inclusive pedagogy can be defined, it may relate to degrees of connectedness: the individual learner being connected into the learning environment; the classroom culture connecting to all learners (Corbett & Norwich, 1999). It is a connective pedagogy which promotes an inclusive school community.

DISCOURSES OF INCLUSION

There are several different discourses which are related to issues of inclusion and exclusion. Fulcher describes the four main discourses on disability as medical, lay, charity and rights, all of which are relevant to the discourse on inclusion. It is important to be aware of changes in emphasis and new terminology in any academic discipline, including that of special education. In 1989, when "Disabling Policies?" was first published, the term, "inclusion" was relatively unused, whilst in 1998, it has become the buzz word in special education.

By the term *discourse* I mean the language used, meanings taken for granted, nuances implied, voices respected, short-hand language codes shared and expressions encouraged among different groups which may be composed of politicians, education and health professionals, parents, disability activists and those who are the recipients of services. Fulcher stresses that discourse determines how issues are talked about, styles of statements and inherently different objectives. Four familiar discourses which will be explored in this unit are those which may be termed as follows: the language of government; the language of learning support practitioners; the language of academic theorists; debates on social exclusion and prejudice in the press. All these examples can be conceived as using languages of common sense, individual deficit and social constructivism or a combination of all three.

A *common sense* discourse is one which uses familiar language and a direct, easily understood style to communicate meanings which convey something of the complexity which is underneath the surface images. It is used in parliament, where many diverse ideas which have roots in extremely complex specialisms are simplified in order to be shared with non-specialists and to be translated into a common code. It is also used in journalism and on television to interpret complicated situations into a form which makes them accessible and interesting to the widest possible audience. This is an inclusive discourse in that it tends to use simple language, direct examples and clearly defined debates. Yet, it is exclusive in its reliance upon structural hierarchies and power relationships which are hidden beneath a surface simplicity.

An *individual deficit* discourse is one which centres upon the problems inherent in the individual and on the ways in which those special needs should be addressed. It tends to focus on syndromes and medical conditions, relating specific clinical causes to behaviour and learning capacity. In many respects, this approach is being encouraged further within an assessment culture which seeks medical labels in order to claim secure funding. This is an exclusive discourse in that it separates out those who need labels from those who do not. However, if it means that each learner is seen as an individual with unique needs which the school or college community should be responsive towards, then this can be regarded as an inclusive and pragmatic discourse.

A *social constructivist* discourse is one which addresses labels like "special needs" within the context of social, political and economic circumstances. The notion of individual need cannot be separated from collective values and deep social structures. Where economic conditions change and employment becomes more precarious, for example, the definition of what constitutes a special educational need will be re-defined to suit the external setting. Issues of what counts as "acceptable" behaviour among pupils are inextricably related to morale in the teaching profession, public perceptions of schooling and government priorities. This is an inclusive discourse in that it rejects notions of the individual being seen in isolation from the collective. Yet, it is inter-related to the discourses of common-sense and individual deficit in that it establishes critiques based upon these specific discourse arenas and their influence.

THE LANGUAGE OF PARLIAMENT

The Green Paper on Special Educational Needs (DfEE, 1997) marks the latest in a line of legislative proposals relating to this area from the early 1980s to the present. It is important for any true understanding of how "inclusion" may be perceived by politicians to listen to their debates, the language they select and the ways in which their feelings are expressed. A close analysis of their discourse can reveal much about how they are conceptualising issues like inclusive educational policy. As Fulcher notes, in relation to the impact of the Warnock legislation, policy at government level does not determine practice but does provide some of the conditions in which developments can occur.

ACTIVITY ONE

Firstly, familiarise yourself with the Green Paper and its relationship to the government White Paper. Note particularly how examples of inclusive educational practice are presented and how inclusion is addressed within the overall discussion.

Then read through the first key reading:

MINUTES OF EVIDENCE

Tuesday 9 December 1997

EXCELLENCE FOR ALL CHILDREN: THE GREEN PAPER ON SPECIAL EDUCATIONAL NEEDS.

If possible, try to supplement this with viewing extracts from television coverage of parliament and newspaper commentary on government provision for special needs.

A politician's use of language is often carefully considered as it is likely to be repeated back to them. In this Activity, it is important to note the language being used and the topics which are given priority in an often tightly structured committee schedule. The costs of printing and typing the Minutes of this Evidence (£450 for printing, £728.53 for preparing from shorthand (footnotes on p.1) indicate that time is money where the business of politics is concerned. So, the topics chosen for close consideration have been selected from many potential other issues to be presented to this sub-committee.

There is an underlying current of obtuseness in the language of parliament, despite the surface simplicity. This is encapsulated on p.5, when Estelle Morris is explaining about the role of the National Advisory Group in forming a response to the Green Paper. She suggests that there are mechanisms and rules of government which might restrict the publication of the relevant minutes. When Mr. Don Foster says, "But within the rules, you are giving us an indication that you would seek to have them published and I am sure we are grateful." the Chairman, Ms. Margaret Hodge, says, "What a wonderful Yes, Minister line!" Within that section (28) is captured the archaic language of parliament (eg. The retention of "chairman", despite the Chair being a woman) and the sense of politicians and civil servants looking from the outside in at their public, media image and at how they can become parodies of themselves.

ACTIVITY TWO

Consider the following questions in relation to the first key reading and, if possible, discuss them within a group:

1) When Estelle Morris refers to "the issue of inclusiveness" as being "one of the strands in the Green Paper" do you feel she is linking special needs issues to broader concepts like basic literacy and numeracy or does she have a specific conceptual framework?

2) What are the main concerns raised about Statementing and how do these relate to the shift of "money that is currently spent in the statementing process to Stages 1 to 3 of the Code of Practice"?

Estelle Morris says (p.5, 30.)

> "So within the first year of coming to Government we now have a situation where provision of early years places in each locality is done in a forum where somebody with an interest or some people with an interest in SEN actually are. I think that that by itself will not bring about earlier identification. Structures do not do that. But if the structure is wrong it makes it more difficult for that to happen, so in that case I am satisfied with that."

This links with Fulcher's contention that government policy can create conditions which influence procedures, although it lacks the power to determine practice. It also relates to the historical approach in "Special Educational Needs in the Twentieth Century" (Corbett, 1998), whereby boundary lines determining what constitutes a learning disability are constantly redrawn at different periods of economic history, according to prevailing political agendas. It is important, as education professionals, to be alert to the significance of structural changes in developing or inhibiting inclusive educational policy and to be critically aware of structures which are ineffective or negative.

In many of the debates on inclusive and exclusive educational policies conducted by academics and disability activists, there are calls to disband those structures which support segregated provision. One of the major obstacles to a comprehensive inclusive provision is that the special school structure with its substantial resource implications exists alongside the support for pupils with special needs in mainstream schooling. This structure was established some years ago with the best of intentions at the time. Once firmly established as an integral element of special education provision, with career pathways and specialist roles for teaching and support professionals, this structure becomes very difficult to dismantle. Where politicians can be responsible for helping to establish structures in the first place, it is clearly vital that these are carefully considered as their long-term effects are significant and can have a wide-reaching impact beyond that which was originally intended.

THE LANGUAGE OF LEARNING SUPPORT PRACTITIONERS

The language of learning support practitioners is essentially practical. It has to be if they are to help in the kind of ways that mainstream staff require of them. One of the main sources of stress and anxiety for busy teachers managing large classes in state primary and secondary schools is coping with any behaviours which disrupt the lesson and prevent them from teaching and the other children from learning. That is why behaviour has become such a contentious issue for teachers and the teaching unions which support and protect their interests.

The learning support teacher has to balance their concern for the individual student whose needs they are addressing with a wider concern for the whole class and their learning experience. This may be regarded as the essence of inclusivity. It is not about that narrow form of integration as defined in the Warnock Report (DES, 1978), which focuses on the physical (locational integration), the interactive (social integration) and the capacity to cope with the curriculum (functional integration). Rather, it concerns the classroom climate. By this, I mean that an inclusive classroom is one which can value and respect individual differences in learning styles, priorities and outcomes whilst working to create a cohesive community with shared goals and a sharing of different strengths. It is this complex balance between individual and collective needs which demands a high level of social skills from the learning support practitioner. The emphasis on pedagogy, assessment procedures and a sharing of expertise only describes part of this job. It is in the means whereby they can soothe anxiety, build confidence and recognise inherent skills in their mainstream colleagues that their support of inclusivity is demonstrated.

One of the characteristic requests of mainstream teachers is for detailed information on "the condition" when a disabled student joins their group. The social model of disability implies that individual special needs are of less significance than collective solidarity and protest against the obstacles which society puts in the way of those who are seen as different in their needs. However, within the practical remit of a learning support teacher, it may be seen as more inclusive to give such help rather than to suggest that the student can be treated the same as all the others and that their specific condition is of no significance. Teachers often feel frustrated and angry if they suspect that they are denied what they see as vital background information which would help them to offer a more focused and sensitive level of support. Within the social context of a school or college community, it may be seen as responsible and an element of active good citizenship to provide excellent information.

Fulcher refers to that professionalism which characterises learning support teachers as being a discourse and its associated practices which makes a claim to expert knowledge and uses language to establish this claim of expertise. I gave examples, in the chapter "Community and the culture of caring", where lay people had taken over the supportive role usually owned by experts. If inclusive education is an unending process, as Booth (1996) implies, then it might be realistic to assume that mainstream teachers (as lay members of a learning support procedure) may gradually come to share in those processes which they currently perceive as the responsibility of special educators.

One of the many difficulties associated with labelling individuals within a specific category is that they rarely fit neatly into one slot only but may have several areas of need. In an educational climate where there are enormous pressures on teachers in schools and lecturers in colleges, it is understandable that the appeal of a ready-made label is considerable. Being able to put a student into a particular category and take out ready-made packages to cater for that category can be comforting. Trying to assess the range of skills which that student may have takes time and concentration, not easy when there are so many competing demands. It is one of the major challenges for a learning support practitioner to ensure that the complexity of student needs are evaluated in a positive way which recognises skills and areas of specific strength.

The case study example selected for Activity Three illustrates the difficulty in labelling. The student being included in a mainstream secondary school has been identified as having Asperger Syndrome, a mild form of autism. He also has areas of exceptional intellectual ability. These place contradictory demands upon the school staff. On the one hand, they needed to provide him with an intensive programme of academic work beyond that of his peers; on the other, they needed to structure a social skills training which was inappropriate for most of his peers. Within these individual needs, they have the challenge of supporting an inclusive classroom culture which can cater effectively for a diverse range of learners, including this specific student who may be vulnerable to bullying. This example has been selected because it helps to illustrate the following aspects of inclusive practice:

1. That the concerns of mainstream staff need to be addressed;

2. That specialist programmes (eg. behaviour modification) may have their valued role within an inclusive provision;

3. That mainstream staff can be taught appropriate skills which enable them to successfully include students who might have been excluded in the recent past.

ACTIVITY THREE

Read Barber, C. (1996) *The Integration of a very able pupil with Asperger's Syndrome into a mainstream School.*

You might supplement this reading with video material on autism or Asperger Syndrome. You may like to address the following questions through group discussion:

1. What does the original Statement of Special Educational Need, issued in March 1988 when he was in Year 4, indicate about the potential dangers of this procedure?

2. In what respects would this particular student present real challenges for staff working with large and diverse classroom groups? Is this kind of behaviour more frightening than some others because it is unpredictable and because his intellectual needs can be demanding?

More children seem to be being diagnosed with Asperger syndrome than in earlier decades. As a specialist in this field says,

> What is Asperger's Syndrome? A few years ago hardly anyone had heard of the term, yet today almost every school seems to have a child with this new syndrome. Yet the first definition of such children was published over 50 years ago by Hans Asperger, a Viennese paediatrician. He identified a consistent pattern of abilities and behaviour that predominantly occurred in boys. The pattern included a lack of empathy, little ability to form friendships, one-sided conversations, intense absorption in a special interest and clumsy movements. However, his pioneering work did not achieve international recognition until the 1990s. Until recently parents and teachers may have realised the child was unusual, but had no idea why, nor knew where to go for help.(Attwood, 1998, p.11)

The linking of a specific syndrome to a set of unusual behaviours can be comforting to parents who are confused and frustrated. It is also seen as valuable by many teachers because it means they can start to treat the syndrome according to the diagnosis.

However, there are significant reservations expressed in relation to such labelling. Parents may actively seek to find a label to explain behaviour which may have a variety of causes. The use of one particular label to define and treat may then preclude other less intrusive forms of intervention. The label may lead to special school placement rather than to inclusion in mainstream. It is important to recall that this case study illustrates how easily inappropriate placements can occur. Had the Statement of Special Educational Needs been implemented in the way in which the specialist professionals suggested, this student would have been placed in a special school outside his locality. This would have been most unlikely to have really addressed either his academic needs or his social inclusion. In holding out for mainstream provision, his parents were trusting that the learning support systems would be able to respond appropriately. Had they failed to do so, the specialist professionals might have told the parents that they only had themselves to blame for going against advice. Such an example of successful social and academic inclusion illustrates that it is worth questioning well-meaning professional guidance if it seems to offer the safe rather than the most satisfactory approach.

One of the changing features of special education is that certain conditions seem more prevalent at particular periods of history than at others. Whereas it was physical disabilities like polio and tuberculosis which were prevalent in the early years of the twentieth century, it is now attention deficit hyperactivity disorder, autism or Asperger syndrome which are among the growth areas of diagnosis. All three medical labels are associated with behavioural problems. These each have a diagnosis which offers a neurological cause. Other behavioural problems among students in schools and colleges are seen to arise from inadequate parenting, poverty and anti-social tendencies. Overall, if teachers were to be asked what were their greatest anxieties in a policy of inclusion it is likely that coping with disruptive behaviour would come at the top of the list. The teacher's unions are also concerned to support colleagues who want to retain the right to exclude exceptionally difficult students. It is important that we recognise that, when we talk about inclusion, it is the challenge of dealing with difficult behaviour which is likely to concern most practitioners more than any other issue.

THE LANGUAGE OF ACADEMIC THEORISTS

Academic language tends to be challenging to read as it is concerned with concepts and arguments, which need to be supported by evidence from relevant literature. Where it is primarily concerned with theory, it can become largely abstract in content and may be difficult to understand. Often the words which academics use are archaic or obtuse, which can serve to alienate the lay reader. Although academic debates are traditionally supposed to be objective, in that they are focusing upon issues and evidence rather than personal feelings, it is hard to separate the individual writer from the ideas being expressed and many would argue that such an attempt at artificially distancing is rarely helpful.

Taking both of the course readers, the ideas being examined are largely at a theoretical level and not based upon empirical research. Both reflect the views and commitments of the authors, based on their personal bias and allegiances. They reflect views in the special education debate but may readily be contested by others with widely different views. This does not mean that they are flawed but that they reflect certain perspectives and values and as such, fail to give equal emphasis to others which another academic theorist might place far higher on their own personal agenda.

The topic of inclusion, as I suggested in the Introduction to this Unit, is one which tends to arouse strong emotions. It is a political issue concerned with fundamental values about equality and justice. Many academics who write about inclusive policy and practice care passionately about the issues they are examining. They are not trying to be objective but to make the case for inclusive education by drawing upon relevant evidence and theoretical argument. Sometimes, they might be expressing perspectives which can be regarded as a form of utopian idealism. Other academic theorists will take an essentially pragmatic approach. Yet others tread a path in between, in which they confront the reality of the schooling context which they see before them and then suggest how this can be approached with the most workable inclusive framework. The example to be examined in Activity 3 is a good illustration of this type.

ACTIVITY FOUR

Read Rouse, M. and Florian, L. (1997) *Inclusive Education in the Market Place.*

Think about the following questions and discuss them with somebody else or in a group, if possible.

1) This paper provides an overview of some of the key theoretical perspectives in the area of integration and inclusive education. Taking the section on "Developments in special education: from integration to inclusion" (pp 324-326) can you highlight 6 of the key theoretical perspectives and put these views into your own words. Include some contrasting perspectives if possible and decide on the key reasons why the authors feel that a policy of including children with special educational needs is being threatened by recent market-place reforms.

2) Consider the concluding reflection that "even in this unsupportive climate, there are schools that are currently demonstrating that inclusion is not incompatible with excellence" (p.334). Select evidence from the debates in this paper which support this statement.

It is useful to reflect on this paper in relation to some of the issues raised by Booth and Ainscow (1998) in their detailed analysis of how teachers can create inclusive classrooms in a range of cultural settings. They stress the importance of imaginative listening, flexibility and visions of equity. Fulcher indicates that teachers are key policy-makers in the complex process of translating legislative discourse into daily practice. In my chapter, "Care with Vision: a new role for professionals" (Corbett, 1998), I indicated that it is possible for professionals in education, health and social services to serve as powerful allies and forceful advocates for the promotion of inclusive community values. Within these varied academic debates, we are all concerned with the central role of teachers and related professionals as potential change agents.

There are distinctive features of style, content and format which mark this third reading out as an academic debate. It relies heavily upon evidence to support argument, rather than saying, "I think this.." although some academic theorists are comfortable in using the first person tense. The use of referencing in the text is particularly effective, linking literature to the arguments without including large quotations which can disrupt the flow. The use of journals like the Times Educational Supplement (p.330) alongside academic books is again valuable in ensuring that current views are discussed.

DEBATES ON SOCIAL EXCLUSION AND PREJUDICE IN THE PRESS

Newspapers can be a rich source of literature in an area like the inclusion or exclusion of pupils with special educational needs. They also reach a far wider audience than that reached by the average academic journal. They tend to give what might be called a "common sense" view. This is because they use the direct and accessible language of journalism to connect with issues which they rightly assume many readers (and parents) are interested to hear more about. These include the following:

a pupil being excluded for attacking teachers / other pupils; parent protests at possible re-enstatements of excluded pupils; schools with higher than average rates of exclusions; school governors who may be in disputes with teachers over exclusions; very young children being excluded for being out of control. The element of drama and crisis inherent in the act of excluding certain learners from schools or colleges has an inevitable appeal to the popular press.

Articles from the tabloid press can be a valuable resource of documentary evidence for research into educational developments. They can compliment academic books and journal papers, providing another dimension to the debates. They have two distinct advantages to traditional sources of academic research material: they offer immediate responses to current events; they provide an insight into the views which the general public are being exposed to in their daily lives. This is particularly important when it comes to research into educational issues like the inclusion or exclusion of certain learners.

As I said in my introduction, inclusive education is an emotional matter about which most people will have strong, gut feelings. The traditional academic approach found in books and journal papers may avoid an emotive style as it is usually regarded as inappropriate. The more dramatic immediacy of newspaper debates allows us, as researchers, to gain a deeper understanding of how attitudes among the general public are formed, fostered and fuelled to give them a distinct picture of what current educational issues are all about.

Whilst academics may regard much journalistic imagery as simplistic and sensational, it is powerful and potent, reaching a scale of audience which the academic debates rarely share. These newspaper articles, therefore, can tell parents how to feel and react when confronted with dilemmas relating to inclusion or exclusion: it is about what might happen in their children's schools and what is happening in the education system. The newspapers speak to them as consumers of education services, helping them to feel that they understand what is going on in schools.

One of the disadvantages of this source of documentary evidence is that it presents education from the bias of the particular editorial base. In this respect, it can serve to confirm already deeply held prejudices among its regular readership. In some of the right-wing tabloids, for example, children from immigrant families are presented as a major source of disruption in schools and poor families are seen as ineffective at controlling their children who are labelled "thugs". Such a reinforcer of widely held views can help their largely right-wing readers feel superior to people who they see as irresponsible, "the undeserving poor" who become a social scourge. The political implications of confirming such stereotypes are clearly dangerous and can only serve to increase social exclusion.

This description of households on a council estate where there was a primary school with major discipline problems gives an indication of this type of journalism:

> The mothers and fathers here blame everyone and everything for what is happening to their children. They never blame themselves. "You would think", retorts a teacher, "that we are bringing up their children for the parents." "We can't do anything with them," one mother complained, "so we rely on the school to do it and they let us down." Yet suggest

> corporal punishment to any of these mothers
> and their claws gleam and their eyes flash.
> "No one is going to hit my child" one said
> menacingly (Levy & Allen, 1998, pp. 16-17).

It is significant that a popular press which has recently demonised children who commit acts of violence is here demonising these mothers. With gleaming claws and flashing eyes, they are presented as extremely menacing and frightening. The middle-classes and aspiring middle-classes are effectively being directed to fear and mistrust the "undeserving poor" who need to be kept firmly in their ghetto. Trying to educate their children is evidently a futile exercise.

Such an article does not help the cause of inclusive education. If anything, it is promoting social exclusion by reinforcing prejudices which help many parents among their readers to feel justified in selecting schools which exclude children whose social and emotional needs may demand high levels of teacher time and effort. The article is helping them to feel that these are not "people like us" but a sub-species who bring their miseries upon themselves. It is almost supporting an attitude which asks, "Why bother to try to educate these children at all? They'll only end up in prison like their fathers." It is in school, moreover, that they meet with other unruly children and create a culture of anarchy and revolt.

In my chapter, "Moral values and public panic" (Corbett, 1998), I reflected that exactly these sentiments now emerging in the popular press were part of the broadsheet backlash of the 1880s, rejecting the value of educating "street ruffians" in the newly formed board schools. The notion of educating the children of the urban poor in industrial Britain was met with considerable opposition in many quarters. This was presented in arguments at the time as creating the following problems: fear of violent, anti-social behaviour in the streets surrounding the board schools; fear that gathering together street ruffians into one building would be dangerous; fear that their learning to read would lead to all kinds of trouble and ultimate revolution; and fear that their parents would keep them at work in the factories and be prosecuted for not sending them to school, leading to increased poverty for the community as a whole. The rallying cry from some detractors of the board school movement was that teaching these children to read and write was to doom them to deep disappointment for it might increase their expectations of social mobility and lead them to want to rise above their station in life. This would then leave a gap in the unskilled labour market which served to underpin social hierarchies.

If we are seriously considering issues of inclusion and exclusion beyond the narrow confines of institutions, it is vital that we relate exclusion from school to broader aspects of community and social values. Those pupils being excluded in the greatest numbers in late 1990s post-industrial Britain are Afro-Caribbean boys. Just as those "street ruffians" of the early board schools were to become factory fodder for the industrial economy, so the slaves from the Caribbean were being brought to Britain to work as servants in prosperous households (forcefully presented in the Spring 1998, BBC 1 serial, "A Respectable Trade"). In this respect, both of these marginalised groups were being perceived as part of the servant class. Social prejudices run deep inside the collective culture of a country. It is not inconceivable that among those white British citizens who continue to perceive all black people as intrinsically inferior are a number of teachers who reflect this social prejudice in their attitudes towards their black pupils. If you really believe that someone is inferior then you will not want them to achieve high expectations.

The reality of social exclusion is that it shows us our least attractive characteristics as a community. It displays our prejudices against anyone who is different from the majority, as reflected in the tabloid, right-wing press. The British National Party was campaigning in the London Borough of Tower Hamlets for the May 7th 1998 local election. Their leaflet, pushed through the door of my house along with those of my neighbours, said that the trouble with the education system in Tower Hamlets was that there were too many immigrant children in schools, which was bringing down standards for all, and the trouble with social service spending was that it was going on things like gay and lesbian support groups which most "decent" citizens did not want. In placing these statements alongside a photograph of an old white man battered and bruised by a gang of Asian youths, the leaflet was implying that the Borough's problems could be directly traced to "outsiders": they used this very word.

Understanding attitudes to social exclusion in education, housing, community resources and employment means confronting prejudice. Many of the general public who read right-wing tabloid newspapers are readily convinced that Britain's problems are due to "outsiders". These "outsiders" may take the form of the "undeserving poor", the latest wave of immigrants, refugees, alienated young people, single parents, gay and lesbian people or disabled people. In the recent outbreak of demonisation of problem children in the press, we need to reflect as readers that the dark side of human nature in general is being conveniently transferred into these "monsters" and "thugs" who can then serve as scapegoats for all the ills of society.

CONCLUSION

In this unit, I have explored the complex debates which relate to educational inclusion and exclusion. In the literature review, it is clear that there is a current emphasis on forming distinctive and positive theoretical models of inclusive educational discourse which take into account both practitioner experiences and the views of disability theorists.

Because discourse is a dominant interest of Gillian Fulcher and myself, I evaluated debates on inclusion and exclusion through a series of different discourse arenas, each reflecting their own priorities. They were representations of the following: the language of parliament; the language of learning support practitioners; the language of academic theorists; debates on social exclusion and prejudice in the press.

Throughout the unit I stressed that in order to understand why inclusion in education is so sensitive an issue, it is important to accept that it involves feelings, values and prejudices. It is not just about who should be included in the classroom and playground but who is inside or outside the dominant discourse arenas within any specific cultural group.

Through reference to the two course readers, I widened the debate to include many varied sites of policy-making and different cultural contexts and their implications for conceptualising inclusion and exclusion.

I noted that the language of government concerns itself with systems, structures and economic viability. Governments in power have to be seen to be doing those things which gain them public approval. Inclusive education is delicate for the government to address. Statementing has proved popular with many vociferous parents, yet it is economically risky in resource, provision and staffing commitments. In deciding to reduce the number of children who are thought to have special educational needs by early years intervention, the government are indicating that the SEN label can be changed to suit changing conditions.

In relation to the questions asked in Activity One, I would suggest that which learners are included or excluded can be changed, not according to severity of special educational need, but according to government priorities in creating new structures and systems.

I suggested in the unit that the language of learning support practitioners has to be practical and accessible to those mainstream teachers whose work they support. In the struggle to gain limited resources the label of a specific syndrome or diagnostic problem has become important again, despite recent resistance from the disability movement towards the medical model of disability. Anti-social behaviour which is difficult to control continues to be the major cause for concern amongst most teachers and creates the largest barrier to inclusion. A Statement may recommend a special school placement for a child with disruptive behaviour precisely because the mainstream teachers may be reluctant to include such an individual. However, such Statements are not always in the best interests of the child concerned and professional views can be challenged.

In response to the questions linked to Activity Two, I suggest that parents as consumers of educational services can opt for inclusive provision, if they are prepared to accept that their decision might exclude them from the kind of support which they might have received had they chosen to be guided by professional advice. The choice is often between situations which are far from ideal but are compromises. In relation to the tensions between different discourse arenas, I suggest that parent power may be said to be on the ascendancy and professional power to be on the wane.

Academic debates on inclusion tend to focus upon two specific aspects: the ways in which inclusion differs from integration as a concept and the implications behind this distinction; the dilemma of promoting an inclusive ideology within a market culture. The issue of school effectiveness is one which is a major cause for concern in current educational research. If an effective school can be shown to also be one which is as inclusive as possible, this may be a way in which an inclusive ideology can adapt to a market culture.

In relation to the questions relating to Activity Three, I suggest that inclusive schools need to be demonstrated to be effective schools if they are to be regarded as successful and viable by politicians and parents.

Newspaper articles about children who are excluded from school tend to focus upon the most dramatic aspects of these events: violence towards teachers and pupils; parents who are also hostile to teachers; out of control children in out of control homes and neighbourhoods. The distorted images can present the excluded individual as a demon, quite divorced from the norm.

Much current intervention in schools is that which takes the behaviour in itself and creates either individual behaviour plans or whole school behaviour policies. The rationale for this is that it is not within the power of schools to do other than control behaviour within their own institution. The new government initiative of addressing the needs of social exclusion zones has expectations that schools will work with other agencies and businesses in their community to raise standards in all aspects of education, training and employment opportunities. Exclusion is presented as a community rather than an individual problem.

In relation to those issues I raise in "Special Educational Needs in the Twentieth Century" I suggest that tackling the issue of social exclusion is about addressing community values of which exclusion from school is just one aspect.

In summary, I want to highlight the following points. Firstly, that different discourse arenas work to their own agendas and priorities, some of which may be competing. Secondly, that fundamental value systems define the extent to which certain marginalised groups will have their needs properly respected. Recognising the contentious nature of conceptualising inclusion, it can only be understood if it is seen as a struggle for equity and civil rights in which there are consistent confrontations with conflicting values and deflecting short-term goals.

REFERENCES

Attwood, T. (1998) *Asperger's Syndrome: A Guide for Parents and Professionals*, London: Jessica Kingsley.

Barber, C. (1996) 'The Integration of a very able pupil with Asperger Syndrome into a mainstream school' in *British Journal of Special Education*, Vol 23, No 1, pp 19 - 24.

Booth, T. (1996) 'A perspective on inclusion from England' in *Cambridge Journal of Education*, Vol 26, No 1, pp 87-99.

Booth, T. & Ainscow, M. (Eds) (1998) *From Them To Us: An International Study of Inclusion in Education*, London: Routledge.

Clark, C., Dyson, A., & Millward, A. (Eds) (1998) *Theorising Special Education*, London: Routledge.

Corbett, J. (1998) *Special Educational Needs in the Twentieth Century: A Cultural Analysis*, London: Cassell.

Corbett, J. & Parker, V. (1998) 'When does an initiative become a commitment?: establishing a secure service for disabled students in a case study of a British university', *Third International Conference on Higher Education and Disability*, University of Innsbruck, July 13-16.

Corbett, J. & Norwich, B. (1999) 'Pedagogy and Learners with Special Educational Needs' in Mortimore, P. (Ed) *Pedagogy and Learning*, London: Paul Chapman.

Department for Education and Employment (1994) *Code of Practice on the identification and assessment of special educational needs*, London: HMSO.

Department for Education and Employment (1997) *Excellence for All Children: The Green Paper on Special Educational Needs*, London: DfEE.

Department of Education and Science (1978) *Report of the Committee of Enquiry into the Education of Handicapped Children and Young People*, London: HMSO.

Fulcher, G. (1989) *Disabling Policies? A Comparative Approach to Education Policy and Disability*, London: Falmer Press.

Levy, G. & Allen, P. (1998) 'Selfish Parents, Spice Girls and Children of 10 obsessed with Sex', *Daily Mail*, Friday February 6, 1998, p 17.

Peters, S. (1996) 'The politics of disability identity' in Barton, L. (Ed) *Disability & Society: Emerging Issues and Insights*, London: Longman Ltd.

Priestley, M. (1998) 'Constructions and Creations: idealism, materialism and disability theory' in *Disability & Society*, Vol 13, No 1, pp 75-94.

Rouse, M. & Florian, L. (1997) 'Inclusive education in the market place' in *International Journal of Inclusive Education*, Vol 1, No 4, pp 323 - 336.

Slee, R. (1998) 'The politics of theorising special education' in Clark, C., Dyson, A. & Millward, A. (Eds) *Theorising Special Education*, London: Routledge.

Social Exclusion Unit (1998) *Truancy and School Exclusion*, report presented to parliament, May 1998.

UNESCO (1994) *The Salamanca Statement and Framework on Special Needs Education*, UNESCO.

UNIT FIVE

TEACHERS, CHANGE AND

PROFESSIONALISM: WHAT'S IN A NAME?

LEN BARTON

INTRODUCTION

This Unit will briefly explore the nature and value of professionalism as an occupational status strategy for teachers. Conceptual ambiguities and contradictory uses of professional identity will be identified and discussed. Viewing teachers as professionals can have both negative and positive benefits. It can be used as a means of control in terms of values and practices as well as a defence mechanism or tactic used by an occupational group against external threats. Importantly, it is viewed as a contested concept needing to be critically engaged with and is part of a more general concern of teachers and other interested parties over a struggle for recognition. Finally, particular implications of the analysis in relation to inclusive education will be drawn out.

In this Unit I will thus briefly consider the following:

- The changing context of educational policy and provision in England in particular.

- Some of the key features of the changes and their impact on the culture and working conditions of teachers.

- The cumulative impact of these developments on the issue of teacher professionalism.

- Implications for inclusive education.

ACTIVITY ONE

Spend some time considering the following questions and write down your thoughts:

- **Do you think you are a professional?**
- **What does 'professional' mean to you?**
- **What factors have influenced your thinking?**

Being taught by a teacher is a fundamental feature of schooling. As pupils we have experienced a range of teachers and teaching styles. Teaching is a topic that many people as former pupils feel experientially qualified to talk about. Thousands of academic books and articles have been published about teachers and teaching. In this Unit we will only be able to briefly discuss a selected number of issues, raise questions and hopefully stimulate further examination and study.

Many voices have expressed various conceptions of what constitutes teaching, for example,

- Teaching is fundamentally a **social** activity. As such it involves the development and use of effective interpersonal skills, sustained interaction and the establishment and maintenance of good relationships. The motivation for this is derived from the belief that teaching can and does make a difference in the lives of pupils.

- Teaching involves the development of a **heightened form of self awareness and critical reflection**. It is about examining our beliefs, intentions and overall effectiveness. Part of this approach is the recognition that as teachers we are also always **learning**.

- Teaching inevitably involves **power-relations**. Thus teacher expectations and interventions can be enabling and positive as well as disabling and disenfranchising. Given the diversity of pupil perspectives and backgrounds this is an extremely serious issue.

- Teaching is intensely emotional and is "infused with pleasure, passion, creativity, challenge and joy" (Hargreaves 1997, p.12). It is much more than being an expert in a particular subject, or competent in particular techniques.

- Globally, teaching is increasingly taking place in a world of limited financial and teaching resources, increasing class sizes, workloads, and in many school buildings which are in need of serious repairs (Harber & Davies 1997).

A range of metaphors have been used to define and discuss the position and work of teachers. At particular periods they have been defined as "agents of social control"; as "missionaries" engaged in the task of civilising and socialising potentially difficult working class pupils, as "jugglers" or "mediators of contradictory expectations" arising from parties representing different values and intentions; as "subversives" representing politically inspired ideologies and agendas; as "change agents"; and finally as professionals whose role-models have historically been those of high status professions such as medicine and law. Such conceptions must not be viewed as necessarily mutually exclusive and some may be simultaneously connected (Grace 1978; Hargreaves 1994; Hoyle & John 1995; Lawn 1996; Woods et. al. 1997).

These brief examples raise some significant issues. Teachers are involved in a struggle for recognition in which the ability to define and maintain particular definitions over, for example, what is the purpose of teaching? What constitutes good teaching? What are the valued outcomes of teaching? Are they part of a struggle within and between different interest groups, including the State? Thus, in relation to teachers, their identity and work, who is doing the defining, why, and whose interests do particular definitions serve, are matters of very serious concern.

Furthermore, at particular historical moments it may be in the interests of different parties, including the State, to represent different and even contradictory perspectives. Thus, attempts by the State to control the educational workforce have involved the application of different strategies ranging from coercive and direct, to more subtle and indirect approaches (Ozga & Lawn 1981; Smyth 1991).

Finally, understanding the position and experience of teachers necessitates not only a careful consideration of micro dimensions such as, biography, school context, ethos and teacher coping strategies, but also, the wider socio-economic conditions and relations within which these factors are influenced and played out. Writing on this issue Fullan (1993) vividly captures the significance of this perspective:

> Making a difference, must be explicitly recast in broader social and moral terms. It must be seen that one cannot make a difference at the interpersonal level unless the problem and solution are enlarged to encompass the conditions that surround teaching...and the skills and actions that would be needed to make a difference. Without this attitude and broader dimension the best of teachers will end up as moral martyrs. In brief, care must be linked to a broader, social public purpose.....(p.11).

One of the key arguments in this Unit is that teaching and the culture of teaching is changing. It is not a static entity. In a Report published by the Organisation of Economic and Community Development in 1990, the changing nature of teaching is clearly articulated in the following ways:

> "The tasks of teachers are today more complex and demanding than in the past. They have to respond to the wishes of parents regarding educational outcomes, the social need for wider access to education, and pressures for more democratic participation within the schools".
>
> OECD Ministers of Education

> "The school teacher's task is increasingly complex and demanding".
> Introduction to the United Kingdom White Paper "Teaching Quality".

"In recent years, in many societies, it has quite clearly been the case that more and more responsibilities have been placed upon teachers, and the role of the teacher has become even more complicated and difficult".

Denis Lawton: Rapporteur to the OECD enquiry on the "Conditions of Teaching" (p.97)

The impact of these changes in England and Wales have not been experienced in a unified way by the teaching force, due to such factors as differing LEA policies, geographical location of schools, parental support, and the gendered nature of teaching. These differential effects are vividly illustrated by what Mac an Ghaill (1992) argues, has been the emergence of a new group of teachers who he calls, the 'new entrepreneurs'. They see the changing situation as an opportunity for acquiring new skills including those of management. Nevertheless, in many staffrooms there is a sense of low-morale, of being undervalued and of having little control over major decisions concerning policy and practice.

Since the publication of the OECD Report the pressures for change have not subsided, but have increased. What factors have been influential in these developments?

THE CHANGING CONTEXT

When considering educational issues we need to recognise that at a national level they are integrally connected to political and economic forces. Education is political in, for example, the sense that it concerns the way a government invests financially in supporting the educational system. This includes, the priorities, values, expectations that have influenced such decision-making. Serious questions need to be asked about such a process. For example, what form and extent of debate took place between all the interested parties? How far will these decisions contribute to combating inequalities or reproducing them? To what extent have the policy-makers endeavoured to both prepare and support key stakeholders for any envisaged change?

A major driving force for change has been the introduction of market-led decision-making. This has been based on a serious critique of existing planning and provision in the sphere of education. In England and Wales, for example, this has included; the condemnation of overly bureaucratic and allegedly politically inspired local authorities, the lack of choice for parents including relevant information on which to make such decisions, the decline in standards of educational achievement and personal discipline within schools, the lack of a significant means of accountability on the part of teachers and schools, the negative need for economic efficiency across the whole system of provision and the irrelevance of much of teacher education courses and a call for, and introduction of, a national curriculum for teacher training (Ball, 1994: Hatcher, 1994; Whitty, 1997; Woodhead, 1997 & DFEE 1998).

The social and economic context in which schools are located is becoming more complex and influential. The impact of globalisation and the interdependency of societies especially in fiscal terms has, and continues to have, impact on the funding, goals, structures and outcomes of educational systems. Schools are increasingly being viewed as quasi-businesses that must compete for pupils and resources. Increased selection and the introduction of new forms of school provision have contributed to the development and legitimation of a highly stratified system of schooling. A new public discourse has emerged which is both accessible and self-evident, in which as Ball (1990) maintains:

> Notions like equality and opportunity have been replaced initially by standards and quality and more recently the ground has shifted again to efficiency and value-for-money (p. 98).

Economic rationality has become a powerful factor in the strategic decision-making at both state and school levels of policy development and implementation.

By focusing on the position and function of schools in relation to a society's achievements in the highly competitive international market-place, fundamental and sustained criticisms have been directed at teachers and their allegedly unacceptable performance. A lack of confidence in schools' abilities to adequately meet these demands has become a perennial challenge to teachers' status and professionality.

The question of the concept 'market' and its application to children and schools is not without its difficulties. For example, in a review essay on 'Educational Markets and School Choice' Dale (1997) contends that a great deal of the work in this area tends to present markets and choice in rather non-problematical ways. This raises a serious issue of how they are defined and the relationships between them. Markets for Dale are always social constructions in which the state is centrally involved in both the forming and regulating of them. The central issue in debates over markets is ".... not the details of how schools are chosen, but the *governance* of education and the role of the state and the market." (our emphasis, p. 454). This necessitates an examination of how funding, regulation and provision are established on a market footing. Markets are not neutral and the establishment of market mechanisms involves the adoption of a new value system in which competitive self interest becomes a priority (Ball, 1994).

ACTIVITY TWO

Read - Myres, K. & Goldstein, H. (1997) *Failing Schools or Failing Systems?*

- **In what ways does your experience within education confirm or raise questions about their analysis?**
- **How does this paper relate to the issue of teacher professionalism?**
- **What is the value of this form of analysis?**

Teachers face new challenges and tasks arising from several important factors. A perennial tension arises from the external imposition of change and its ownership within schools and the ability and responsibility of teachers to develop innovatory policies and practices. The changing nature of work and the abilities of teachers to prepare pupils for this experience. The decreasing pupil motivation for those pupils who are particularly vulnerable in a world of limited job opportunities. Increasing pupil diversity, expectations and needs within a work culture in which the support systems are not able to adequately meet such demands. The information technology revolution with digital television, the Internet, Cyberspace, which create difficulties of control over the form and extent of knowledge which pupils bring into school.

The process of learning and the relationship between teacher and pupils will become increasingly challenging in this changing context. Finally, the position of schools and teachers in terms of the function and relationship between parents and the community. This becomes an increasingly difficult issue in contexts in which governments attempt to use parents to control teachers.

Discussing the frantic pace, extreme scope of change and the breadth of legislative powers used by Government in support of such interventions, Hargreaves (1994) maintains that:

> More than anything, ... it is extreme in the disrespect and disregard that reformers have shown for teachers themselves. In the political rush to bring about reform teachers' voices have been largely neglected, their opinions overridden, and their concerns dismissed. Change has been developed and imposed in a context where teachers have been given little credit or recognition for changing themselves, and for possessing their own wisdom to distinguish between what reasonably can be changed and what cannot. (p. 6)

A central proposition of Hargreaves' analysis is that the problems and challenges which increasing numbers of teachers face are to be understood in relation to the wider socio-economic context in which schools are placed. Within this context teachers face increasingly difficult and contradictory pressures. These include the expectation to contribute to the task of economic regeneration, to help rebuild national identities including cultural and political factors and to undertake these fundamentally urgent concerns in a context of serious financial restraint.

Thus, for Hargreaves, 'ideological compliance and financial self-reliance have therefore become the twin realities of change for many of today's schools and their teachers' (p. 5).

Teacher professionalism faces threats from the impact of marketisation, intensification and routinisation of the work culture within schools. One of the most serious threats has come from the impact of casualisation on the teaching body. Teacher redundancies have been extensive and the Government proposed changes to pension arrangements resulted in a rush of staff to retire (Wallace, 1997). Older, experienced staff have been replaced by less expensive and experienced teachers. The use of supply staff on both short and long term bases, some supplied by private companies that have emerged in recent years, further exacerbates this problem. Non-union policies are often promoted through this process.

The topic of professionalism and how it is conceived often makes it difficult to distinguish between whether it is an aspiration or an actuality. We have no agreed universal definition or understanding of key terms. Attempts to do so are thus expressions of a struggle to redefine the work of teaching by a range of external bodies, including governments, and by teachers themselves. The literature offers insights that are both paradoxical and contradictory with professionalism being depicted as being strengthened in some cases and reduced in others. It is this which has encouraged Hargreaves and Goodson (1996) to also highlight a distinction which is reflected in the literature:

> .... between *professionalisation* as a social and political project or mission designed to enhance the interests of an occupational group and *professionalism* as something which

defines and articulates the quality and
character of people's actions within that group
(p. 4).

In a survey of the relevant literature they maintain, that it may be more appropriate to view some aspects of teachers' work as being *reprofessionalisation* in terms of its greater complexity and in others *deprofessionalisation* in terms of teachers' limited decision-making over actual goals and purposes.

Placing the issue of professionalism within the more general context of community regeneration and the learning society, Nixon *et al* (1997) argue that former relationships and values relating to the professions no longer have currency. They maintain , that a new set of professional codes are needed which will integrate the various relationships and practices that teachers now need to be involved in, in new and exciting ways.

They examine some of the key assumptions underlying the traditional model of professionalism in which they contend, specialist knowledge and expertise are conceived in essentially static ways. Supporting the position of Hugh and John (1995) they argue, that an attempt to determine whether teachers are professionals according to certain absolute criteria, is now a fruitless task. For them, it is the issue of control and power that is crucial, including such questions as: "Whose interests do professionals control and who has power over their exercise of that control" (1997, p. 9).

```
ACTIVITY THREE

Read - the paper by Nixon, J., Martin, J., McKeown,
P. & Ranson, S. (1997) 'Confronting "Failure":
Towards a Pedagogy of Recognition.'

•  To what extent do you see the issue of 'failure' as
   central to the topic of professionalism?

•  How valuable is their conception of a 'new
   professionalism'?

•  What issues does this paper raise for you in your
   teaching situation?
```

INCLUSIVE EDUCATION

Inclusive education is about encouraging ways of thinking and relating to one another in which the dignity and well-being of all pupils and staff is of paramount importance. It arises from an antagonism and dissatisfaction towards the social divisiveness, exclusivity and elitism of the prevailing system of educational provision and practice. Inclusion is concerned with openness, engaging with difference in dignified ways and necessarily raises questions about current conceptions of what schools are for and whose needs schools serve.

This approach to education is much more than a question of access. It is about providing welcoming institutions and the removal of all forms of policy and practices of exclusion. Education for *all* as expressed in what Kemmis (1994) terms 'the socially just schools' involves a relentless and serious commitment to the task of identifying, challenging and contributing to the removal of injustices. Part of this task necessitates a self-critical analysis of the role schools play in the production and reproduction of barriers of exclusion in their varied form.

Learning to live with one another in a non-oppressive way involves the pursuit of a new politics of difference and diversity. These now represent a challenge, a means of generating change and an encouragement for people to question unfounded stereotypes, hostility, prejudice and discrimination.

A traditional model of professionalism encouraged detachment, dependency on the part of clients and self-interest. It is hardly a suitable model from which to engage with these new demands and changes. Supporting a particular view of professional identity could well be counter-productive and alienate teachers from those in whose lives they claim to benefit. This has been most powerfully articulated by Ginsberg (1997) in the following way:

> Adopting professionalism as a model for educators' engagement with/in communities may be inappropriate because of the undemocratic teaching within many versions of the ideology, not only to distance teachers from parents, students and other members of the community, but to establish a hierarchical relation between professionals and the lay public (p. 8).

Within the field of special education criticism of low expectations on the part of teachers, of constructing and legitimating disabling categories and labels and pursuing policies and practices that serve the interests of teachers, than those of the pupils are illustrative of the inappropriateness of such an approach (Tomlinson, 1982; Barton & Tomlinson, 1984 and Barton, 1986).

What is needed is a new vision, a new identity, that is not distant, impersonal and dependency-creating, but one which is seen as being supportive and collaborative, in which teaching to diversity and the empowerment of all learners are recognised as essential hallmarks of an inclusive perspective and ethos.

CONCLUSION

The extent to which we believe the education of our future citizens to be of paramount importance will have a significant consequence with regard to how seriously we view the question of teacher professionalism.

In terms of making a difference in the lives of such pupils, the position of the teacher is of paramount importance. Teaching is more than a set of competencies, techniques, or expertise in appropriate forms of knowledge. Professionalism has to be understood not in terms of the establishment of barriers of demarcation, exclusivity and elitism, but rather inclusive, democratic and collaborative characteristics. The discourse surrounding the issue of professionalism can be both enriching and debilitating and thus there is no room for complacency.

A serious consideration of the topic of this Unit is both urgent and necessary especially in connection with the deliberations concerning the issue of inclusive education. This will involve the examination of such key questions as:

- What do we expect of teachers?
- What are their rights and responsibilities?

- What support do they need to undertake their work effectively?

- How does gender and race impact on teacher experience?

I hope this Unit, although brief and selective over its aspects of consideration, will have provided sufficient stimulus for you to examine these issues in greater depth. The emphasis is upon *your* perspective, understanding and vision.

So, I now conclude with my final question - Professionalism - What's in a name?

REFERENCES

Ball, S. (1990) *Politics and Policy Making in Education,* London: Routledge.

Barton, L. (1986) 'The Politics of Special educational needs' in *Disability, Handicap & Society,* Vol 1, No 3, pp 273-290.

Barton, L. & Tomlinson S. (Eds) (1984) *Special Education and Social Interests,* London: Croom Helm.

Dale, R. (1997) 'Educational Markets and Social Change' in *British Journal of Sociology of Education*, Vol 18, No 3, pp 451-468. (Review Essay).

DFEE (1998) *Teaching: Higher Status, High Standards*, London: DFEE.

Fullan, M. (1993) *Change Forces. Probing the Depths of Educational Reform,* Lewes: Falmer Press.

Ginsburg, M.B. (1997) 'Professionalism or Politics as a Model for Educators Engagement within Communities' in *Journal of Educational Policy,* Vol 12, No 1/2, pp 5-12.

Grace, G. (1978) *Teachers, Ideology and Control,* London: Routledge & Kegan Paul.

Harber, C. & Davies, L. (1997) *School Management and Effectiveness in Developing Countries. The Post-Bureaucratic School,* London: Cassell.

Hargreaves, A. (1994) *Changing Teachers, Changing Times: Teachers' Work and Culture in the Post-modern Age,* London: Cassell.

Hargreaves, A., & Goodson, I. (1996) 'Teachers' Professional Lives: Aspirations and Actualities' in Goodson, I. & Hargreaves, A. (Eds) *Teachers' Professional Lives,* London: Falmer Press.

Hargreaves, A. (Ed) (1997) 'Rethinking Educational Change: Going Deeper and Wider in the Quest for Success' in Hargreaves, A. (Ed) *Rethinking Educational Change With Heart and Mind,* Vancouver: Association For Supervision and Curriculum Development.

Hatcher, R. (1994) 'Market relationships and the management of teachers' in *British Journal of Sociology of Education*, Vol 15, No 1, pp 41-62.

Hoyle, E. & John, P.D. (1995) *Professional Knowledge and Professional Practice,* London: Cassell.

Kemmis, S. (1994) 'School Reform in the '90s: Reclaiming Social Justice'. Paper is obtainable from the Institute for the Study of Teaching, The Flinders University of South Australia, Adelaide.

Lawn, M. (1996) *Modern Times? Work, Professionalism and Citizenship in Teaching,* London: Falmer Press.

Mac an Ghaill, M. (1992) 'Teachers' Work: Curriculum Restructuring, Culture, Power and Comprehensive Schooling' in *British Journal of Sociology of Education*, Vol 13, No 2, pp 177-197.

Myres, K. & Goldstein, H. (1997) 'Failing Schools or Failing Systems?' in Hargreaves, A. (Ed) *Rethinking Educational Change with Heart and Mind.* Vancouver. Association for Supervision and Curriculum Development.

Nixon, J., Martin, J., McKeown, P. & Ranson, S. (1997) 'Confronting "Failure": Towards a Pedagogy of Recognition' in *International Journal of Inclusive Education,* Vol 1, No 2, pp 121-141.

OECD (1990) *The Teacher Today,* Paris: OECD.

Ozga, J. & Lawn, M. (1981) *Teachers, Professionalism and Class,* London: Falmer Press.

Smyth, J. (1991) ' International Perspectives on Teacher Collegiality: A Labour Process Discussion Based on the Concept of Teachers' Work' in *British Journal of Sociology of Education*, Vol 12, pp 323-346.

Tomlinson, S. (1982) *A Sociology of Special Education*, London: Routledge & Kegan Paul.

Wallace, W. (1997) 'Let Me Out, I'm a Teacher' in *Times Education Supplement.* 17-1-97 (Features pp. 4-5).

Whitty, G. (1997) 'Creating Quasi-markets in Education: A Review of Recent Research on Parental Choice and School Autonomy in Three Countries' in Apple, M. (Ed) *Review of Research in Education*, Vol. 22 (Washington, DC: AERA).

Woodhead, C. (1997) 'We Must Take Back Our Schools' in *Reader's Digest,* February, pp 49-54.

Woods, P., Jeffrey, B., Troman, G., & Boyle, M. (1997) *Restructuring Schools, Reconstructing Teachers,* Buckingham: Open University Press.

UNIT SIX

TEACHERS, CHANGE AND PROFESSIONALISM IN ENGLAND
AND WALES: PROFESSIONAL DEVELOPMENT FOR
DIFFERENCE OR DIFFICULTY?

HAZEL BINES

INTRODUCTION

This unit will be concerned with the changing role of teachers in the light of social, educational and policy orientations towards an inclusive approach to education. It will examine the developing role of teachers whose work and careers are associated with pupils deemed to have special educational needs and the changes required of all teachers to develop inclusion. It will consider in particular the implications of changing perspectives, roles and responsibilities for both initial teacher training and continuing professional development and will include examination of some key policy documents in relation to policy and provision for special educational needs and both general and specialist training. A number of assumptions about training needs and models will be challenged and it will be questioned as to whether current frameworks and expectations in relation to such training will actually support inclusive models of schooling.

The unit will start with an historical overview, to put present debates and policies on roles and responsibilities into context. It will trace in particular the way the roles of teachers designated as particularly concerned with children with difficulties have developed over the last twenty years since the publication of the Warnock Report in 1978. There will be a particular focus on the development of an advisory, cross-curricular and collaborative approach to working with subject and class teachers in mainstream settings. The first exercise will then focus on the training implications of such conceptions of roles.

The middle part of the unit will consider the range of current and probable future policies in relation to special educational needs and education in general. There will be a particular emphasis on possibilities and constraints in relation to inclusion. The second exercise will be concerned with the identification of current and future training needs in relation to such policies.

The final section will review government approaches to initial training and continuing professional development, both in general and in relation to special educational needs. It will focus in particular on the new standards for such training and whether they match current policy contexts and tackle the issues raised in the previous two sections. The exercise related to this section will involve a critique of training proposals from the Teacher Training Agency.

A core theme of this unit will be that inclusion challenges notions of 'special' and 'ordinary' teachers and that both will have to change to implement inclusion effectively.

The unit will use the terminology 'special educational needs' (special educational needs) as a descriptor for particular forms of provision and teaching, in line with current policy and professional usage. However, it is recognised that such terms do reinforce the perceived differences between pupils, provision and professional expertise which are also the subject of critique in the unit. They should therefore be seen in such a light.

THE REDEFINITION OF ROLES AND PROVISION

THE DEVELOPMENT OF 'SPECIAL EDUCATIONAL NEEDS'

The starting point of this section is the Warnock Report on special educational needs (DES, 1978). Looking back over twenty years it is difficult now to recognise the importance of this report at the time to those who were working in special education. However its impact was considerable. Firstly it redefined categories of special need, laying the ground for a range of subsequent legislation and policy based on such a redefinition. Secondly, it brought together in one policy document the different strands of provision in special education, namely remedial provision in mainstream schools and the separate system of special schools. Finally, as the first major report concerning special educational needs since the 1944 Education Act, it was perceived as having the potential to introduce an enhanced level of national policy interest in relation to special educational needs and a new commitment towards developing provision. This was very important to those working in this field at the time, since as will shortly be discussed, both mainstream remedial and special school provision were neglected in, and marginal to, the general development of education.

Although this is not one of the formal exercises, you might find it useful to look at the Warnock Report as an important historical document, and compare what it says about different aspects of provision to their development today, including issues of professional training.

As suggested above, special educational needs provision at the time of the Warnock Report was essentially two-fold. It comprised what was then called 'remedial teaching' in mainstream primary and secondary schools and a separate system of special schools, each one concerned with a particular category of special educational needs, including learning, behaviour, sensory and physical categories.

The new definition of 'special educational needs' put forward by the Warnock Report brought these two elements of provision together in policy terms. It was designed to replace in particular the different categories associated with special schools but it also had the effect of redefining 'remedial education' as an aspect of 'special educational needs'. This was reinforced further by the Warnock Report's contention that up to one in five pupils might have a special educational need at some time during their school career. Given that the Report suggested that some 2% of such pupils might need a statement of need, and that most of such pupils were more likely to be in special schools, this meant that some 18% were to be found in mainstream schools. This was perceived as recognition at last of the range of educational needs in mainstream schools which had been covered by 'remedial education'. The Report also gave some support to integration and to conceptualising special educational needs as a 'continuum' of needs, which also laid the basis for a more unified approach to special educational needs across both mainstream and special schools.

THE REDEFINITION OF PROFESSIONAL ROLES

The professional impact of such ideas was considerable, particularly in relation to remedial education. The Warnock Report, and the 1981 Education Act which succeeded it, both encouraged and legitimated the development of new approaches to such education. For example, members of The National Association of Remedial Education (NARE) (now part of NASEN, the National Association for Special educational needs, which is the main professional organisation of teachers who identify themselves as particularly concerned with special educational needs in the UK) had already begun to debate in their journal Remedial Education the limitations of current approaches to provision and the development of a broader role for remedial teachers. This focused on several elements.

a) the need to take a more preventive approach to learning and other difficulties by changing the curriculum and teaching methods in mainstream classes

b) reconstructing the role of remedial teachers to support such preventive work

c) developing a more central and important role for remedial teachers within the school in order to reduce the separation and marginalisation of remedial provision.

Such developments were aptly characterised by Golby and Gulliver (1981) as developing remedial education from an 'ambulance service' towards 'consultancy on road safety'. Remedial teachers would still provide some support, particularly in relation to the basic skills of literacy and numeracy, but would also spend time working with colleagues in secondary subject departments and primary classes. Their role was to advise on the modification of curricular content and teaching approaches in order to give pupils greater access to the mainstream curriculum and to reduce the difficulties experienced by some pupils associated with inappropriate teaching materials and approaches.

Such debate then crystallised into a number of recommendations on the ideal role of remedial teachers (NARE, 1979; Gains and McNicholas, 1979). This redefinition of role was also accompanied by a growing number of examples of putting such a redefinition into practice (e.g Ferguson and Adams, 1982).

The adoption of the term 'special educational needs' following the Warnock Report also had an influence on this redefinition. It soon replaced 'remedial' as a descriptor for pupils, provision and teachers, and the debate about redefinition of role was reconceptualised further in terms of teachers of 'special educational needs' (e.g. NARE, 1985). Reflecting the growing development of a cross-curricular, advisory and preventive role, such teachers gradually became 'co-ordinators' of policy and provision, which in turn led to the almost universal adoption of the current descriptor of 'special educational needs co-ordinator' for those teachers with teaching and managerial responsibilities for special educational needs in mainstream primary and secondary schools. Managerial aspects of the role were also increasingly defined as central, with special educational needs co-ordinators taking responsibility for the development of school policies on special educational needs, for the deployment of teaching staff and classroom assistants related to special educational needs, and for the development of learning resources. The legitimacy of having a central role within the school was also reinforced by notions of the special educational needs co-ordinator as a general 'learning consultant' holding a unique position and capacity to contribute to curricular, pedagogical and organisational school development and evaluation (Dyson, 1990, 1991).

This current conception of the special educational needs co-ordinator role thus represents a considerable shift from the isolated remedial teacher of basic skills prior to the Warnock Report. It has also been accompanied by a slower, but equally significant redefinition of the role of teachers in special schools. This has not focused so much on advisory or co-ordinating roles within the school, since the prime role of the special educational needs teacher in the special school remains that of class teacher. However, it has involved a more coherent approach to managing and developing curricular and other provision within the special school as a whole and the gradual adoption, particularly with the introduction of the National Curriculum, of the curriculum framework of mainstream schools. It has also involved a broader role for special schools, in particular that they should work more closely with mainstream schools to support the integration of pupils in mainstream schools who might formerly have been educated exclusively in special settings (Ashdown et al, 1991; Baker and Bovair, 1989, 1990).

In turn, the role of special educational needs support services has also been redefined in the same way, with teachers working in such services now being required to offer a range of support to mainstream schools in particular. This may include advice on pupils experiencing particular difficulties in ordinary classes and the provision of more specialist support for pupils with particular needs as part of their integration from segregated settings into mainstream schools.

The last twenty years since the publication of the Warnock Report has therefore seen significant changes in the roles of teachers concerned with special educational needs. These can be summarised as:

a) a more unified conception of the special educational needs teacher, less dependent on the location than previously, which stresses in particular that there is considerable commonalty of role and expertise across both the range of special educational needs and the variety of mainstream and special settings and services

b) an extended and more important role for such teachers, encompassing curricular, pedagogical and organisational developments in both mainstream and special schools.

In turn, the roles and responsibilities of all teachers have changed. Firstly, the broader, cross-curricular role of the special educational needs teacher presumes that class and subject teachers will work collaboratively with special educational needs staff in order to improve provision for all learners. Class and subject teachers are also expected to exercise a range of responsibilities in relation to pupils considered to have special needs. The 1981 Education Act, for example, laid down the expectation that all teachers should play a role in the identification of needs. The assumption that some 20% of pupils may present one or more special needs at some time during their school career indicates that most pupils with such needs are likely to be in mainstream classes and settings, taught primarily by ordinary class and subject teachers. In turn, access to the National

Curriculum for all pupils is based on the expectation that class and subject teachers in both mainstream and special settings will plan and provide for learning within such a framework and therefore have a considerable responsibility for developing appropriate curricular approaches, including differentiation of content and teaching methods to respond to particular needs. This means that there has been an important shift in emphasis. Far from responsibility for teaching children identified as experiencing difficulties being located with a specialist teacher, all teachers are considered responsible for teaching all the students in their classes. Delegation of budgets which include an element for special educational needs to mainstream schools also presumes that schools will take considerable responsibility for planning and provision. The Code of Practice for special educational needs, and accompanying legislation and guidelines emphasise strongly how mainstream schools in particular should develop their responsibilities for special educational needs, including drawing up a whole school policy, implementing particular stages of identification and intervention, encouraging partnership with parents and with other professionals, and evaluating the effectiveness of the school's work in relation to special educational needs (DfE, 1994; Ofsted, 1996, 1997). Reports from the Audit Commission and HMI have also emphasised the importance of mainstream schools increasing their capability for providing for special educational needs (Audit Commission/HMI, 1992a, 1992b).

IMPLEMENTING NEW ROLES

However, the implementation of such roles and expectations has been problematic in several respects. Although the special educational needs co-ordinator role in particular is now recognised as both important and legitimate, the development of the cross-curricular, advisory and support role remains limited in a number of ways. In part, this is due to insufficient staffing, so that not all teachers and pupils can expect or receive such support in every classroom and subject. This is particularly true of primary schools where the special educational needs co-ordinator is also usually a class teacher and therefore can only work with colleagues at times outside the teaching day. However the role has also been difficult to implement because of other constraints. These include class and subject teachers' constructs of special educational needs, their concerns about their expertise in relation to special educational needs and the workload involved in developing more appropriate provision, and their attitudes towards having teaching and other support in their classrooms (Bines, 1986, 1993). Constraints on the developing role of special school and support service staff are similar, with the added difficulties of having to develop collaborative work across different institutional settings. And although the introduction of a National Curriculum has established a common curricular framework and language for working with all pupils and teachers, the inflexibility of many aspects of the National Curriculum and associated assessment, and the increasing pressures on schools to demonstrate rises in pupil achievement, have undermined the potential of greater integration of both educational settings and the nature of pupils' learning experiences. Changes in school funding under LMS have also had an impact on the provision of support services, with many being reduced in size and remit, or subject to market decisions by schools to purchase such services, leading to restricted opportunities to facilitate and support change (Copeland et al, 1993; Lunt and Evans, 1992).

Equally, the extent to which subject and class teachers feel able to fulfil new expectations is questionable. Both research and more anecdotal professional experience suggest that teachers still regard special educational needs as being primarily "someone else's problem" and feel they lack sufficient expertise and time to plan and teach effectively for the range of special educational needs, particularly given the limited support available from special educational needs teachers. Some also find it difficult to work in a collaborative way, feeling that the special educational needs teacher may be impinging on their 'territory' when it comes to particular subject expertise or pedagogical approaches (Bines, 1986, 1993). Constant curricular reform, such as the implementation of the National Curriculum, has also affected the expertise and time which teachers are able to give to developing a more differentiated approach to curricula and pedagogy. The implementation of a market approach to education has also generated new pressures on teachers and schools to focus on the higher range of pupil achievements in order to enhance the school's 'market image' (Bowe and Ball, 1992). Finally, changes in the content of initial training courses, coupled with increasing demands on teachers, have left many teachers feeling ill-prepared to provide effectively for the range of pupil needs in schools (Garner, 1996).

TRAINING IMPLICATIONS

On the one hand therefore, there has been a considerable development in the role of special educational needs teachers which in turn has generated a considerable amount of thinking about the expertise now required of special educational needs teachers. However this has not been matched by developments in the approach, expertise and training of most class and subject teachers. Indeed, although familiarisation with aspects of special educational needs is part of initial training, other pressures on the training curriculum have reduced the time now given to developing knowledge and experience of the diversity of pupils' learning and teaching approaches. Subsequent opportunities for staff development are then often limited to new curriculum initiatives which may not encompass issues in relation to special educational needs. There are also very few opportunities for engagement with more critical analysis of policy, to consider, for example, how the curriculum and organisation of schools may contribute to defining some pupils as "having special educational needs".

Above all however, training has focused on developing and extending the expertise of the special educational needs teacher, including both managing the cross-curricular, advisory, 'whole school approach and more recently, the numerous requirements of the Code of Practice. Training in relation to special educational needs is still conceptualised largely as training of specialist special educational needs teachers. It is then the special educational needs teacher's responsibility to provide staff development for subject and class teachers as part of the 'whole school' approach. Some aspects of the special educational needs role are also not given sufficient priority. There may be too much emphasis on learning about particular pupil needs when a large part of the role involves interpersonal and organisational expertise. It is also a policy role, concerned with changing attitudes and priorities (Bines, 1988). It therefore remains questionable whether training has changed to match the redefinition of roles and provision discussed above.

ACTIVITY ONE

Now read:

Bines, H. (1992) "Developing roles in the new era" and Dyson, A. (1991) "Rethinking roles, rethinking concepts: special needs teachers in mainstream schools" both from the NASEN journal Support for Learning. These articles summarise some of the debate about roles and raise a number of questions about training from which you should consider:

1. Is new expertise required by such approaches, from both subject and class teachers and those particularly concerned with the teaching of children who experience difficulties? And if so, what expertise?

2. What particular training might then be required to develop such expertise?

3. Are such approaches and such training likely to break down or reinforce ideas about pupil differences?

EXCELLENCE AND INCLUSION?

DEVELOPING INCLUSION

This section will focus on current and future policy in relation to special educational needs and subsequent implications for training. The key text here is the recent government Green Paper (DfEE. 1997) which identifies a number of policy initiatives in relation to special educational needs. These include:

♦ early identification and intervention
♦ improvements in literacy and numeracy
♦ school improvement and target setting
♦ enhanced partnership with parents
♦ improved professional development
♦ modifications to the current Code of Practice for special educational needs
♦ support for inclusion.

Support for inclusion is seen to involve pupils from special settings being educated in mainstream schools but with continuing specialist provision where needed. It is also seen as part of the drive to raise standards of pupil achievement in all schools.

However there are a number of questions in relation to the implementation of such intentions. For example, current government policy is particularly concerned with the raising of standards of achievement. However the notion of 'standards', linked to targets which pupils and schools should meet, is not very compatible with the acknowledgement of diversity and difference (Bines, 1998). Although changes are being made, we also still have an inflexible National Curriculum and associated assessment which presumes that pupils will learn certain content and progress towards certain levels of achievement. Again that would seem to suggest that diversity and difference are not truly recognised.

Provision for special educational needs is also being developed in an educational market based on delegated management, which has generated competition between schools for pupils and their associated funding and which is forcing schools to consider their market position in terms of pupil achievement. In turn, there is increasing competition within schools for resources and a tension between providing effectively for all pupils and developing a market position based on high standards of pupil achievement (Bowe and Ball, 1992). Such pressures are also reinforced by Ofsted inspection which fails to recognise the variations in pupil intake and resources and the impact of social and other disadvantage on pupil achievement and progression.

This does not provide a facilitative framework for prioritising inclusive policies. In particular, current concepts of the curriculum and associated pupil achievement have a profound effect on teachers' constructs of educability and in particular, of special educational needs. Normative standards almost inevitably suggest that those pupils who do not achieve them are not only different but have learning or other difficulties when compared with such norms. This is relevant to both pupils in mainstream settings and to pupils in special settings, some of whom were completely ignored by the original National Curriculum which even in its lower Key Stages assumed certain knowledge, skills and experience which not all pupils will necessarily have at the age presumed.

In addition, other aspects of government policy are reinforcing such problems. For example, the new literacy and numeracy hours are based on particular pedagogical approaches which may not be appropriate for pupils with learning difficulties. They include, for example, an emphasis on whole class teaching which may not suit the learning styles of all pupils and which may make it difficult to differentiate teaching approaches to respond to this and other learning differences between pupils.

The current organisation of most classrooms, levels of staffing and the range of learning and other resources also does not easily facilitate curricular and pedagogical approaches which can respond effectively to pupil differences. With classes of over 30 pupils in many schools, the individual teacher is pressured to teach to what is considered 'average' levels of knowledge and skill. There is not time, in relation to preparation or within the classroom, to develop materials and teaching approaches which can take account of diversity and respond in different ways. This again reinforces the conception that differences are difficulties when such difficulties are actually generated by systematic failure to provide for difference.

Finally, many of the organisational features of schools often compound such difficulties. For example, curricular and pastoral systems may not be managed in a way which encourages a unified approach to pupils' needs. Or management may be hierarchical in nature, which may work against the more collaborative ethos seen to be required to develop more inclusive approaches. Above all, there is increasing evidence to suggest that the market approach to education, and pressures towards increased accountability, are engendering a managerialist approach towards education which is shifting attention away from the curriculum and teaching methods towards administration and management. This may be particularly true of special educational needs teachers who, because of the requirements of the Code of Practice and other initiatives, are being reconstructed as managers, a trend which is emphasised further by conceptions of the role which focus on organisational and managerial change within schools (Bines, 1995).

IMPLICATIONS FOR PROFESSIONAL DEVELOPMENT

Such issues are particularly important in relation to professional training and development. The range of professional development provision seen to be required to implement the government's policy (DfEE, 1997) is identified as including:

* standards in initial teacher training which ensure that all newly qualified teachers will understand their responsibilities under the Code of Practice, can identify children with special educational needs and can differentiate teaching practice appropriately

* a supported induction year in which newly qualified teachers can develop further their knowledge and skills, including in relation to special educational needs

* a range of professional development provision which will encourage teachers to develop further skills in curriculum planning, teaching and assessing pupils in relation to special educational needs

* a qualification for special educational needs specialists, based on national standards, including both generic aspects and specific elements related to particular special educational needs

* national standards for headteachers which focus on setting targets for improvement, monitoring and evaluating the quality of teaching and learning, and motivating and enabling teachers, all of which are relevant to special educational needs

* improved training for special needs assistants

* further training for school governors

* changes in the role of educational psychologists so that they spend less time on formal assessment and more time on supporting and advising schools.

The above are not particularly contentious in that the range of professionals involved is identified and an increase in training provision would undoubtedly be welcome, particularly for groups such as learning support assistants and governors. However such plans are very general in nature. There also needs to be more consideration of the realities of implementing inclusion and the difficulties involved in changing schools (Clark et al, 1997). Further thinking is also required in relation to the nature of inclusion. It still tends to be regarded as reform of special educational needs provision rather than as change in mainstream schools (Dyson and Millward, 1997). If we are to have inclusive education however, some fundamental changes will have to be made in schools and in current government policies. For example, schools will have to be allowed to design much more flexible curricula and their performance will need to be judged in different ways from the current emphasis on normative test results.

ACTIVITY TWO

Consider the policies outlined in the Green Paper in relation to inclusion and the associated training needs and then consider:

a) what new expectations of teachers are raised by the government's most recent policies in relation to special educational needs?

b) what kind of professional development opportunities will need to be developed in order to realise such expectations?

PROFESSIONAL DEVELOPMENT FOR INCLUSION?
MODELS OF TRAINING

Your responses in the exercises for Sections 1 and 2 will have depended on the range of your reading and experience and your particular perceptions of the training implications of government and other policy initiatives. It is likely however that you will have identified a range of knowledge and expertise, and associated professional development agendas, for both special educational needs and class and subject teachers. Views on these do vary but models are likely to include the following elements:

* knowledge of particular special educational needs
* identifying and assessing needs
* curriculum planning and implementation
* differentiation
* classroom management.

In addition to the elements of individual expertise identified above, models of training also usually recognise the importance of various personal qualities and skills to facilitate teachers working collaboratively in schools. For special educational needs co-ordinators in particular other training needs are also identified, such as organisational and administrative skills, knowledge of finance and resources and the ability to deploy a range of personnel and other resources. They are also seen to need the knowledge and skills associated with advisory support and staff development.

All of the above are important in relation to developing effective curricula and teaching approaches. However, there are other important aspects of training which will be necessary to develop inclusion, such as values and attitudes and the capacity to analyse critically educational policy and provision. If it is the case that inclusion depends on substantial changes in schools as a whole, then professional development also needs to be directed towards enabling teachers to develop such change, through analysis of provision, policy development, collaborative working and careful evaluation. Different types of professional development for teachers in different roles may also be needed. For example, for those entering teaching, training may include establishing the principle of inclusion, the importance of recognising and providing for diversity as a matter of equal opportunities and rights, and the ways in which teachers can develop their expertise to meet such ends. For experienced teachers, training will probably have to concentrate more on changing assumptions about pupil differences and the role of the teacher, in order to change current approaches based on normative assumptions about pupil achievement.

Professional development for inclusion would therefore seem to require a different vision of teacher professionalism. Current models tend to regard teaching as a series of prescribed knowledge and technical skills to which a few additional elements can be added in order to extend capability in relation to a wider range of learning needs. Inclusion however requires an engagement with values, policy development, collaborative working and analytical evaluation. Policies to implement inclusion will therefore have to be accompanied by a very different approach to teacher professionalism and training.

BEYOND SPECIALIST SPECIAL EDUCATIONAL NEEDS TEACHERS?

If we are to think more radically about inclusion, we will also need to move away from a model which emphasises the specialist role of the special educational needs teacher towards one which emphasises the role of all teachers within schools which are committed to providing for diversity. The professional development of special educational needs teachers will therefore have to change. In particular, if inclusion is seen as a change in mainstream provision, the focus of training must inevitably be the most effective ways of changing the nature of schools. Various forms of expertise may continue to be important, but the special educational needs teacher's role will also require the capacity to analyse schools in order to make them more inclusive. Policy development, as well as curricular and pedagogical support, would then be an important part of training. The logic of inclusion also suggests that special educational needs teachers should also be trained to critique reliance on themselves.

Such ideas are not new. Early debate on the development of support and advisory role implied that specialist teachers should be working towards their own extinction by developing effective curricula and pedagogy in schools. However the notion of special educational needs was not fully challenged. Rather the aim was to make every teacher a 'special' teacher through sharing of specialist knowledge and expertise in order to adapt curricula and teaching methods. Inclusion, on the other hand, presumes a more radical approach. Rather than adaptation and difference, the curriculum, and teaching approaches, should respond to, and realise, diversity.

CURRENT POLICY: TRAINING FOR DIFFERENCE OR DIVERSITY?

We will now consider current policy on 'training', from the Teacher Training Agency.

Over the last two years, the Teacher Training Agency (TTA), the government body concerned with standards and funding for both initial and in-service training of teachers, has been developing a range of new standards for different stages of teaching. For initial training it has developed both a range of standards and a National Curriculum which now apply to all initial training courses. In addition it is developing standards for continuing professional development, including for headteachers, subject co-ordinators and special educational needs co-ordinators.

ACTIVITY THREE

You should now read the TTA's Standards for special educational needs co-ordinators and consider the following:

a) How far do these standards match your own views of qualities and expertise?

b) Do they support current trends in policy in relation to special educational needs, particularly policies which refer to 'inclusion'?

c) Are there any particular limitations or weaknesses in the way standards and training are approached in this document? In particular, will they reinforce or change current conceptions of pupil difference?

Again your comments will depend on your particular reading, experience and views. I would however like to make several points about these standards. For example:

a) There is a focus on basic and other skills which reinforces traditional notions of the 'special educational needs teacher' and 'pupils with special educational needs'.

b) There is a concern with technical skills rather than the ability to work effectively and collaboratively with others in varying school contexts.

c) The pressure of accountability on the special educational needs co-ordinator rather than the school as a whole, reinforces the notion that special educational needs are primarily the responsibility of the 'special educational needs teacher' rather than the whole school.

d) Most importantly of all perhaps, very little consideration is given to the need for the special educational needs co-ordinators (or other special educational needs professionals) to have to change educational values and practice in more radical ways if inclusion is to be effected.

e) Such plans are developed in isolation from the crucial importance of training for **ALL** teachers to extend both their concepts of educability and their approaches in the classroom.

CONCLUSION

We began this unit with a consideration of the redefinition of special educational needs and the role of special educational needs teachers. Such redefinition promised a more flexible and interactive concept of special educational need and changes in schools to make them more able to respond to the diversity of pupils. There have been some changes in approaches, not least that it is more widely recognised that curriculum and organisation in schools do affect pupils' learning opportunities and that schools need to change in order to become more inclusive.

However 'training' is still directed towards traditional skills and qualities and towards divisions of labour between special educational needs and class or subject teachers which will continue to reinforce ideas of 'specialist' expertise and most importantly, of pupils' 'needs' and 'difficulties' rather than difference and diversity. As noted in other units, we will have to engage with social and political ideas, as well as educational beliefs and technical expertise, in order to develop inclusion. You might like to conclude this unit by considering briefly the range of professional development you would develop to support such fundamental changes.

REFERENCES

Ashdown, R., Carpenter, B. and Bovair, K. (1991) *The Curriculum Challenge: Access to the National Curriculum for Pupils with Learning Difficulties,* London: The Falmer Press.

Audit Commission/HMI (1992a) *Getting in on the Act: Provision for Pupils with Special Needs: The National Picture,* London: HMSO.

Audit Commission/HMI (1992b) *Getting the Act Together: Provision for Pupils with Special Needs: A Management Handbook for Schools and LEAs,* London: HMSO.

Baker, D. and Bovair, K. (1989) *Making the Special Schools Ordinary? Vol 1,* London: The Falmer Press.

Baker, D. and Bovair, K. (1990) *Making the Special Schools Ordinary? Vol 2,* London: The Falmer Press.

Bines, H. (1986) *Redefining Remedial Education,* London: Croom Helm.

Bines, H. (1988) 'Equality, community and individualism: The development and implementation of the 'whole school approach' to special educational needs' in Barton, L (Ed) *The Politics of Special Educational Needs*, London: The Falmer Press.

Bines, H. (1993) 'Curriculum change; the case of special education' in *British Journal of Sociology of Education*, Vol 14, No 1 pp 75-90.

Bines, H. (1995) 'Special educational needs in the market place' in *Journal of Education Policy*, Vol 10, No 2, pp 157-171.

Bines, H. (1988) 'The national context' in Davies, D. and Garner, P. (Eds) *Managing Special Needs in the Mainstream School: The Role of the special educational needs co-ordinator*, London: David Fulton.

Bowe, R. and Ball, S.J. with Gold, A. (1992) *Reforming Education and Changing Schools*, London: Routledge.

Clark, C., Dyson, A., Millward, A.J. and Skidmore, D. (1997) *New Directions in Special Needs*, London: Cassell.

Copeland, I., Ayles, R., Mason, H. and Postlethwaite, K. (1993) 'LEA support for special educational needs pupils: two years on from the 1990 SENNAC survey' in *Support for Learning,* Vol 8, No 2, pp 43-50.

DES (1978) *Special Educational Needs (The Warnock Report)*, London: HMSO.

DfE (1994) *The Code of Practice for Special Educational Needs*, London: DfE.

DfEE (1997) *Excellence for All Children*, London: DfEE.

Dyson, A. (1990) 'Effective learning consultancy: A future role for special needs co-ordinators?' in *Support for Learning,* Vol 5, No 3, pp 116-127.

Dyson, A. (1991) 'Rethinking roles, rethinking concepts: Special needs teachers in mainstream schools' in *Support for Learning* ,Vol 6, No 2, pp 51-60.

Dyson, A. and Millward, A. (1997) 'The reform of special education or the transformation of mainstream schools?' in Pijl, S.P., Meijer, C.J.W. and Hegarty, S. (Eds) *Inclusive Education: A Global Agenda,* London: Routledge.

Ferguson, N. and Adams, M. (1982) 'Assessing the advantages of team teaching in remedial education: the remedial teacher's role' in *Remedial Education,* Vol 17, No 1, pp 24-31.

Gains, C.W. and McNicholas, J.A. (1979) (Eds) *Remedial Education: Guidelines for the Future*, London: Longman.

Garner, P. (1996) 'A special education? The experiences of newly qualifying teachers during initial training' in *British Educational Research Journal* , Vol 22, No 2, pp 155-164.

Golby, M. and Gulliver, J.R. (1981) 'Whose remedies, whose ills? A critical review of remedial education' in Swann, W. (Ed) *The Practice of Special Education,* Oxford: Blackwell.

Lunt, I. and Evans, J. (1991) *Special Educational Needs under LMS,* London: Institute of Education.

NARE (1979) *Guidelines No 2 The Role of the Remedial Teacher,* Stafford:NARE.

NARE (1985) *Guidelines No 6 Teaching Roles for Special Needs,* Stafford: NARE.

Ofsted (1996) *The Implementation of the Code of Practice,* London: Ofsted.

Ofsted (1997) *The Special Educational Needs Code of Practice: Two Years On,* London: Ofsted.

Teacher Training Agency (1998) *National Standards for Special Educational Needs Co-ordinators,* London: TTA.

UNIT SEVEN

THE CONTESTED CURRICULUM

CHRIS WINTER

INTRODUCTION

I have written a unit about curriculum in this module 'Difference and Difficulty' within the Inclusive Education course because I believe that curriculum plays a key role in constructing difference and difficulty in education. This will be the focus of the unit. However, curriculum is not a straightforward concept. The term curriculum can be understood in a number of ways. Whatever meaning you give to the term, it remains at the heart of teaching and learning.

ACTIVITY ONE

How do you understand the term 'curriculum'?

Write down your own meaning of the word, together with examples.

In this unit, I ask you to consider the idea of curriculum in four different ways. In the first of these, curriculum is described as course content or a syllabus. The second takes this idea further by including educational experiences described in school documents. The third involves a view of curriculum as an educational proposal which is translated into practice.

In the fourth approach, which I adopt in the unit, curriculum is understood to be a selection of knowledge which is always underpinned by assumptions about what knowledge is of most value. According to this fourth, broader view, curriculum embodies certain features, for example: a certain way of looking at student knowledge and at student learning; a view of the sort of society it is hoped the curriculum will produce; an idea about who the audience will be for the curriculum.

This fourth view identifies curriculum as representing moral, philosophical and political ideas and also a tool which has a powerful influence on learners. Through curriculum, messages about knowledge, values, skills and culture may be transmitted to students. These messages are powerful agents by which ideas can be passed on from one generation to the next. That is not to say that these messages are always taken up and accepted unproblematically by students: in some cases, this does occur, but in others, students contest and resist curriculum messages.

In this unit, I introduce several ideas and ways of thinking about curriculum theory and curriculum practice. Some of these are difficult to understand and involve some hard thinking. I remember when I encountered for the first time one of the ideas I will be introducing to you later in the unit for myself. This occurred when I was studying for my own Masters degree in Educational Studies with the Open University. I found the concept of 'discourse' extremely difficult to understand - it took me two years of mental struggle and many hours of reading and searching in dictionaries and texts for an explanation! So, do not be put off by some of the ideas presented here. Instead, test them out through your own experiences and ask colleagues, other students on the course and tutors to discuss their understanding of the ideas with you.

In this unit, curriculum is treated as an assemblage of messages (a discourse) representing positions of power. I will consider how the state may form one of several influences on curriculum by producing, circulating, negotiating and transmitting beliefs. Some of these beliefs become dominant in society. Curriculum messages are communicated to students by the learning process which operates through symbols. Each learner constructs curriculum messages in her or his way according to their way of looking at the world.

These ideas form the theoretical framework of the unit. They will be returned to in more depth during later sections of the unit. In the next section, I will look in more detail at the different ways of thinking about the curriculum and how each approach can be viewed critically.

CURRICULUM: A CONTESTED CONCEPT

The literature gives a wide range of ways of understanding and defining the term curriculum. A popular dictionary definition is 'a course of study' which some people think of in terms of course content or a syllabus. The current National Curriculum statutory orders (DFE, 1995) for children aged 5 - 16 are such written texts detailing the knowledge content of the ten subjects prescribed for teaching in primary and secondary schools in England and Wales. Two problems of this content approach to understanding curriculum are: first, that, by concentrating on subject content, all the other experiences which students have of school, for example, interaction with other students and teachers; the ethos of the school with its value systems and moral order and activities, such as assemblies, after school clubs and school productions, are excluded from the definition, when these actually play an important part in students' experiences of school. Second, given the developments in understanding of the nature of knowledge and its changing form (Blenkin, Edwards and Kelly, 1992, p 2), the question of what knowledge is of most worth arises, suggesting that a selection of knowledge content which is justified as 'educationally sound' may not be as straightforward as it may seem.

A second view of curriculum includes those educational experiences which extend beyond the content of subjects to include those identified within the formal documents of the institution, such as the School Development Plan, the Mission Statement, department handbooks, policy statements and the school prospectus. The problem with this view of the curriculum is the gap between the written policy and curriculum practice as it actually exists. For example, a school may circulate to parents a policy statement against bullying, detailing the aims, intentions and purposes guiding and informing it, but at the same time, if this policy is not implemented and bullying occurs in the school, then the theory does not correspond with the practice. This distinction represents the difference between the 'formal' or 'official' curriculum as contained in documents and the 'informal' or 'unofficial' curriculum as it is experienced by students in the school.

Lawrence Stenhouse provides a third definition of curriculum in which the relationship between policy and practice is emphasised:

> A curriculum is an attempt to communicate the essential principles of an educational proposal in such a form that it is open to critical scrutiny and capable of effective translation into practice
>
> (Stenhouse, 1975, p 5).

ACTIVITY TWO

1. Read the Stenhouse definition of curriculum closely. Analyse it by writing a paragraph which explains what it means to you.

2. Compare the meaning of the word 'curriculum' you gave in Activity 1 with the definition given by Stenhouse.

By looking more closely at the Stenhouse definition of curriculum it is possible to enquire into issues around the concept in more detail. Stenhouse challenged the view of curriculum as a tangible object, a list of content, a statement of aims or plan, and instead portrayed the curriculum in terms of a **relationship** between a principled educational proposal and its practice. He overcame the problems of the 'theory - practice' divide by describing curriculum as a process of communication which relates proposals to 'effective practice'. Thus, theory was transformed into practice through the process of social interaction. Curriculum, according to Stenhouse is not fixed and adequate, but available for critique and change. This understanding of curriculum as provisional allows us to see the curriculum, not as a fixed, immutable text, but as a socially constructed phenomenon, designed to achieve certain 'educational' purposes in particular places at particular times in history.

However, by dwelling on the idea of the 'essential principles of an educational proposal', does Stenhouse neglect to consider those unplanned effects of teacher activity we understand as the 'hidden curriculum' of implicit values which are excluded from official documents and which may not even be consciously recognised by teachers and students? Here I refer to the subtle and covert messages which are transferred through everyday practices and interactions in school. An example of this is the way in which teachers interact differently with boys and girls in the classroom. Robinson's research in Tasmanian high schools and colleges demonstrated how teaching methods and classroom practices around discipline were influenced by teachers' stereotyped attitudes towards masculinity and femininity (Robinson, 1992). She found that teachers' traditional perceptions of femininity governed their views about how girls 'should' behave in class and when girls were assertive, loud, confrontational and aggressive, they were considered to be 'bad' or 'difficult' girls although boys displaying the same behaviour were dismissed as 'naturally boisterous' (p 280).

Related to this is the issue of the 'received' curriculum or the way in which students understand and make their own meaning out of their experience of the curriculum. This is an essential element of the process of education as it involves the interpretation of the curriculum on the part of the people for whom the curriculum is designed and constructed. Since students are complex human beings with a range of cultural experiences and pre-existing knowledge which they bring with them into the classroom, it may be important to consider the curriculum according to **their** experience and understanding of it. George Riseborough summarises this idea of the students as curriculum constructors:

> Thus the lesson does not simply belong to the teacher, children can and do make it their own. They put so much on the agenda of the lesson, to a point where, they are the curriculum decision makers. They make a major contribution to the social

> construction of classroom knowledge.
> Children actively select, organise and
> evaluate knowledge in schools. Further,
> lesson time is not solely the teacher's time,
> it is 'stake and site of class struggle'
> (Riseborough, 1985, p 214).

Is the built environment of the school part of the curriculum? To what extent does the physical space of the school reflect the nature of the curriculum? (Armstrong, 1999a, forthcoming). In one school where I have carried out research in the past, large classrooms were originally built 30 years ago to accommodate groups of students who were engaged in learning within an integrated curriculum, through group work and individual enquiry. At this time, tables were arranged in groups and different groups carried out different tasks. The physical structure of the building and the arrangement of classrooms were designed to meet this curricular need. Lessons were longer than today and there was little need for movement from class to class, so corridors were built narrow. With the introduction today of a more prescribed knowledge based curriculum consisting of separate subjects and less coursework there has been a move in the school towards more transmissive, whole class teaching. In response, large classrooms have been divided into two separate rooms with rows of tables and chairs allowing students to face the front of the class. Narrow corridors now prove to be a problem for the large scale movement of students which occurs more frequently than in the past as students transfer from room to room six times a day to learn the separate subjects of the National Curriculum.

If it is acceptable to state that teachers' social interactions with students form part of the curriculum, can I then argue, that, since teachers' interactions with students are underpinned by their professional belief systems, I may include teacher conceptualisations of students into a definition of curriculum? Chessum (1980) enquired into teachers' perceptions of 'disaffected' students' behaviour in her research and her analysis showed how teachers drew on certain conceptualisations to explain the behaviour of 'disaffected' students as a result of the institutional constraints under which the teachers work. The inevitable moral and political conflicts which arise in school between teachers and students force teachers to conceptualise behaviour in certain ways in order to cope with 'disafffection'. In Chessum's research, teachers drew on family pathology explanations for 'disaffected' behaviour as these were most accessible and appropriate in terms of their professional and organisational interests and immediate operational concerns.

I am now in a position to construct a definition of curriculum which allows enquiry into the concept in more rigorous and critical way:

> Curriculum may be understood as a series of principled educational proposals susceptible to change and open to questioning but which are constructed on the basis of a selection of knowledge. The concept includes the ways in which social life is organised within the context of the school built environment as well as the whole range of experiences of teachers and students. Curriculum is embodied within the school culture, signalled and transmitted through spaces, texts and social interactions and involves messages about what knowledge and cultural practices are valued. The notion extends to embrace the ways in which teachers and students conceptualise knowledge of subjects and persons as these govern the nature of their social interactions. These interactions are underpinned by ideologies which may

operate to include or exclude students and
in this way, students may be encouraged to
engage with, or students may be
marginalised from, the experience of
curriculum.

In drawing attention to a certain selection of knowledge, curriculum may
be seen as a social construct representing a **political** judgement about
what knowledge and cultural practices are valued. The word political is
used here to denote how power is controlled and distributed: in other
words, who gets what, where, why and how? In the process of
constructing curriculum, five important curriculum questions arise which
further demonstrate the political nature of the process of curriculum
construction:

What should be taught?

Why should it be taught?

How should it be taught?

To whom should it be taught?

How is it understood?

If some groups of students learn most effectively when the curriculum is
organised in a certain way, for example, if it emphasises the links
between subjects; if it involves the local cultural history of the
community; if it encourages active citizenship, is student - centred and
responsive to student learning needs, then these groups may be
educationally empowered as learners through the curriculum. The same
groups may find learning separate subjects consisting of content far
removed from their daily lives and cultures, in an ethos of competitive
individualism, less educationally empowering. In other words, if the

notion of 'political' involves who gets what where and when, then it is clear that from these curriculum questions, education, and, in particular, the curriculum are political and should never be regarded as 'neutral', god-given or objective. As a selective experience of knowledge, pedagogy and assessment, for students who are organised on a particular basis according to a particular purpose, curriculum represents a political force responsible for maintaining or transforming knowledge and cultures by embodying them with power and status. Moreover, as a political tool, a curriculum is more likely to reflect the knowledge, values and culture of more powerful groups in society than less powerful groups (Hamilton, 1990, p 38).

CURRICULUM AS DISCOURSE

One way of conceptualising curriculum which allows an understanding of it as a contested and political project is to draw on the work of Foucault and post structuralism. According to this perspective, curriculum represents an example of a power-knowledge formation in which knowledge and power are inextricably interconnected. Truth does not exist outside of relations of power. This perspective involves looking at curriculum as a message system in which positions of power are deeply and subtly embedded as described earlier (p 2). Foucault challenged the way of thinking in which knowledge is seen as separate from power and the claim that the acquisition of truth and knowledge uncontaminated by power is the means by which an individual can achieve liberation (Usher and Edwards, 1994, p 85). Instead, he argued for an acknowledgement of the centrality of power in the construction of ways of knowing. Power-knowledge formations in post structural thinking are exercised within discourses, the second central notion in Foucault's thinking.

Discourses are:

> practices that systematically form the
> objects of which they speak.....Discourses
> are not about objects; they constitute them
> and in the practice of doing so, conceal
> their own invention.
>
> (Foucault, 1977, p 49).

In viewing discourses as representations of dominant 'ready made syntheses' of knowledge, Foucault called for us to deconstruct them and to probe the spaces which remain after their construction in order to understand that which is 'already said' or 'never said' (Foucault, 1972, p 25). By doing this we can expose discourses as influences of power on our thinking by shaping:

> .....what can be said and thought, but also
> who can speak, when and with what
> authority. Discourses embody meaning
> and • social relationships, they constitute
> both subjectivity and power relations.
>
> (Ball, 1990, p 2).

In this sense, then, curriculum may be understood as discourse, allowing us to deconstruct and explore the political positions embedded within as well as those which are absent in order to understand better how power is exercised within the school curriculum.

One source of political power in the curriculum has arisen recently through the increase in state intervention in the education system. In one school in which I have carried out research, the power of the discourse of the Humanities curriculum was very different in the school in the early

1970s compared with the mid 1990s (Winter, 1997). During the 1970s, the control of the Humanities curriculum discourse lay more with the teachers in terms of construction and development than with the state. Today, with the introduction of a state prescribed discourse of a statutory National Curriculum in England and Wales, with firmly defined GCSE and 'A' Level criteria and national standardised assessment, the state exercises more determining control over the curriculum in this school. Foucault's post structuralism is useful because it allows us to pose some questions about this: what discourses were and are involved in constructing the curriculum? What part has the state played in bringing about change? What relations of power underpin the changing discourse of the curriculum?

CURRICULUM AND THE STATE

Although, in the past, the State has adopted a laissez faire attitude towards education (Carr and Hartnett, 1996, p 72), more recently, it has come to play an increasingly important role in the curriculum of schools (Hall, 1981, p 12, Ball, 1990, p 8). Any discussion of power relations and the curriculum should therefore include reference to the State. It would be useful, therefore, to look at how we may understand the State. Green (1990) understands the State to be:

> not only the construction of the political and administrative apparatus of government and all the government controlled agencies which constitute the public realm but also the formation of ideologies and collective beliefs which legitimate state power and underpin concepts of nationhood and national character
>
> (Green, 1990, p 77).

This definition extends an understanding of the State beyond the formal and concrete State institutions and organisations of government to include those abstract ideas which may be held by and shared with the state arising from groups in society which are not contractually linked to the apparatus of State itself. In pushing the definition of the State to encompass 'ideologies and collective beliefs', Green punctures the notion of a neat and unproblematical definition of the boundary between the State (political society) and civil society (private and public institutions). In a similar way, Gramsci before him presented a picture of the relationship between the State and civil society as fluid, sometimes seeing the two as separate, sometimes as one, but drawing attention to the dialectic by which the State is constructed and reconstructed through social interactions.

Green captures the significance of State as process in his understanding of the State as 'an active, organising force in modern societies' (Green, 1990, p 92) and Apple (1996, p 52) confirms this process-focused view of the State: '....at all levels, the State is *in formation'* (Apple's italics). Gramsci (1971) himself defines the State as:

> the entire complex of practical and theoretical activities with which the ruling class not only justifies and maintains its dominance, but manages to win the active consent of those over whom it rules (Gramsci, 1971, p 244).

HEGEMONY

The strength of Gramsci's theory of the state and its relationship to civil society lies in the insights it gives into the complex process of ideological transformation occurring between and within the state and civil society, bringing about a degree of conformity to the ideological position of the dominant power and hence perpetuating existing social relations. This process of transformation involves **hegemony**, a complex activity operating within and between social groups as they interact and communicate on an ideological basis. The process is a dynamic one, involving the continual negotiation towards the objective of consensus. But a permanent consensus is never reached, instead a temporary settlement emerges which represents a provisional ideological balance of power in favour of the dominant group. A continuous activity of conflict and agreement takes place with the creation of alliances, the attempted incorporation of subordinate groups by dominant groups and the articulation of some of the interests of the subordinate groups by dominant groups, as long as these do not damage the ideological project of the dominant groups. Apple describes the hegemonic process as:

> ..... a process in which dominant groups in society come together to form a bloc and sustain leadership over subordinate groups. One of the most important elements that such an idea implies is that a power bloc does not have to rely on coercion.....rather, it relies on *winning consent* to the prevailing order, by forming an ideological umbrella under which different groups who usually might not totally agree with each other can stand. The key to this is offering a compromise so that such groups feel as if their concerns are being listened to.... but without dominant groups having to give up

their leadership of general social tendencies.

(Apple, 1996, p 14/15).

ACTIVITY THREE

Read Apple, M. J. (1996) *Cultural Politics and Education*, **Buckingham: Open University Press, Chapter 3, pp 52 - 67**

In the extract, Michael Apple gives an account of a conflict over a text book series chosen by teachers to be used in a local school district in an area of the USA he calls 'Citrus Valley'.

1. Apple sees the text book as, amongst other things, 'the fundamental curriculum artefact in classrooms' (p 53). To what extent do you believe this statement to be true in your experience?

2. What is the role of the state in the story Apple tells about Citrus Valley? To what extent, in your opinion, did the state 'increase the potential for rightist movements to grow'?

So far in this unit, we have looked at ways of understanding curriculum. Through critiques of these approaches we have developed an alternative, broader definition which encompasses, among other things, the curriculum as a politically powerful force. We have considered the role of the state within the process of curriculum control and have studied one view of how beliefs and value systems may be promoted and rejected in society through the hegemonic order. One aspect of curriculum process we have neglected so far is the **manner** in which curriculum messages may be transmitted to students and teachers. We may assume that this occurs through an unproblematical process we understand as 'learning', but there exists a theory which may help us to understand the learning process as a subjective and collective meaning making exercise. This theory, developed by George Herbert Mead (1934) is known as symbolic interactionism.

SYMBOLIC INTERACTIONISM

Symbolic interactionism is a conceptual framework for understanding social interaction as the means for forming group and individual identity and behaviour through meanings arising out of relationships between people (Blumer, 1962). It focuses on individuals as constructors of meaning and the continuous process of negotiation around meanings within particular social contexts like schools, providing a means of understanding the ways in which students and teachers think and act. The theory is founded on three basic premises. The first is that people act towards things on the basis of the meanings that the things have for them. The second premise is that the meanings of such things is derived out of the social interaction between people. The third is that the meanings are interpreted by people in their interactions with the things they encounter.

Before this theory was developed it was believed that social actions arose out of factors operating on a person to produce some predictable behaviour outcome. Mead refuted the idea that people possess minds which are 'given' and fixed, that they live in a world of 'pre-existing' and 'self constituted objects' which stimulate them to respond in certain predictable ways (Blumer, 1971, p 11). He saw people as having 'selves' which, by operating self reflectively, allow them to make indications or interpretations of the physical and social world in which they interact. This means that a person's line of action may not be predictable or obvious, but, instead reflects her or his subjective interpretation of the experience. Writing about Meads' work, Blumer says:

> The process of self interaction puts the human being over against his (sic) world instead of merely in it, requires him (sic) to meet and handle his (sic) world through a defining process instead of merely responding to it, and forces him (sic) to construct his (sic) action instead of merely releasing it (1971, p 12).

According to symbolic interactionists the social world is constructed through interpersonal negotiations around the meanings conferred on everyday objects in everyday experience. An object is a human construct, 'constituted for the meaning it has for the person ..... for whom it is an object' and the meaning of the object 'arises from how the person is initially prepared to act towards it' (Blumer, 1971, p 14). Human actions are derived from the meanings objects have for them. By defining and interpreting each other's acts as objects, in other words, by 'taking the role of the other', the action of individuals in a group come to fit together in what Blumer calls 'joint action' (p15).

What is the relevance of this theory to a study of curriculum? If we understand the school curriculum as object, in other words, curriculum as an assemblage of messages representing a range of experiences for students, it has different meanings for individual students. These meanings are derived from social interactions between students, teachers, texts, classrooms, posters, belief systems and behaviours .... in fact the whole range of 'objects' constituting a school curriculum. The responses of students to curricula experiences reflect the meaning those experiences have for those students. Students define and interpret each others' acts and the acts of teachers as objects and it is on the bases of these that their own meaning making, subsequent action and self identities are founded.

In some cases, curriculum as object represents a positive experience for students. One student may construct her or his experience of the curriculum as empowering and liberating. However, another student may construct the same curriculum as a negative experience which is oppressive and disempowering. It may deny her or him the opportunity to learn how to think autonomously, how to gain the required qualifications or how to collaborate creatively. In the three case studies which follow, different curriculum scenarios will be described. Each one forms the context for curriculum as object. When you come to read them, it may be useful for you to think about the sorts of social interactions students may be subject to, the interactions they contribute to and how these interactions may be understood by students.

The relationship between the school curriculum and the state in the recent past in England and Wales provides a valuable basis on which to explore how relationships between different social groups are being maintained, reproduced or transformed through the curriculum. Although it was the Education Reform Act of 1988 which introduced the mandatory subject-based National Curriculum into schools in England and Wales it would be unfair to look at this content-based curriculum alone, without broadening the view to include the range of educational reforms which accompanied it and interacted with it. This way a fuller picture of the relationship between the school, the curriculum and society may be explored.

Since the ERA (1988), the alliance of the New Right and, more recently New Labour has implemented a prescribed and centralised National Curriculum and associated standardised testing; the delegation of budgets to schools; open enrolment; published examination results; a decline in the control of the Local Educational Authorities and the introduction of a technical/rational approach to management in schools. Underpinning the new curriculum and assessment procedures is a stereotypical view of the 'normal' student: one who performs at a certain level according to his or her age, engages with a positivistic view of knowledge compartmentalised into traditional subjects and learns according to the pre-ordained behavioural objectives of the National Curriculum Orders.

Thus, the power of the notion of the 'normal' student has intensified under the rule of the New Right hegemonic alliance and has been continued and enhanced under the New Left. The National Curriculum consists of a selection of knowledge for students to learn irrespective of their culture and community and irrespective of the interests, specialisms and professional discretion of their teachers. Standardised and criteria-led testing involves measuring students against a 'norm'. Thus, the dominant ideology surrounding the 'norm' is expressed through the curricula of schools via the teaching, learning, rules, tests, profiling and social interactions of everyday practices operating in schools. Control of this situation is maintained by a juxtaposition of a the neo-liberal 'freedom' for schools to make decisions 'independently' about how to spend their delegated budgets and organise their schools within the neo-conservative context of strong state control of the curriculum and assessment system which are in turn driven by the competition of the market place. In order for schools to survive, levels of performance have to be maintained to produce a respectable position in the league table in order to ensure future recruitment. In addition, the decline in LEA control of schools has meant that a layer of decision making and a wider view of policy making at local level (often involving a re-interpretation of national policy to suit local conditions) has been marginalised, leaving individual schools more vulnerable to national policy. The final change is the introduction of a technical managerialism which understands education, not as a complex, value-laden and moral activity aimed at the intellectual and cultural empowerment of a diversity of people towards a more democratic future, but as a technical and rational business, based on the principles of the market place.

195

ACTIVITY FOUR
Read Whitty, G., Power, S. and Halpin, D. (1998) *Devolution and Choice in Education: The School, the State and the Market,* **Buckingham: Open University Press, Chapter 6, pp 79 - 93.**

Questions:
1. Read about the changes which the rise of the 'evaluative state' (p 87) have brought about at the institutional level. These, according to Whitty, Power and Halpin include:
- **reordering of authority structures**
- **more goal oriented-relationships between staff and students**
- **emphasis on assessment and accountability diminishing the quality of teaching**
- **teaching becoming more standardised and superficial**
- **emphasis on student attainment rather than student learning**
- **marginalisation of non-assessed curriculum areas**
- **organisation of teaching groups in streams rather than mixed ability**

Is there any evidence of these changes in the institution in which you work or used to work?

It is within this political and historical context that the notion of the 'entitlement curriculum' has been placed, to offer to all students a so-called 'equality' of experience through a common core curriculum. But, as we have already seen, curriculum is political; it reflects the values of those who construct it. If those values are far removed from the values of those students who are expected to learn from it, or the values of the parents, family, neighbours and peers, then it will be difficult for those students to accept the curriculum and learn from it (Kelly, 1990, p 96).

Such a curriculum denies the existence of class, race, ethnicity, gender, religious and geographically based differences in the interests, values and cultures of students in schools (Carr and Hartnett, 1996, p 173). It presents teachers with the problem of teaching students a curriculum which may not make connections with the realities of their lives and denies them the opportunity to learn about topics which may be meaningful, purposeful, stimulate their interest and curiosity and empower them as members of society. The existence of a common core curriculum does not account for the differences and diversity of students and their communities and makes it difficult for teachers to celebrate the 'educational significance of students' culture and of wider cultural repertoires' (Carr and Hartnett, 1996, p 173).

The following three case studies have been selected to demonstrate curriculum messages as representing powerful positions in their relationships with students. Curriculum as a political phenomenon may serve to include or exclude students from the experience of education.

CURRICULUM CASE STUDIES

CASE STUDY ONE: ALPERTON COMMUNITY SCHOOL, ENGLAND

Armstrong (1998b) (forthcoming) describes how teachers in the ethnically mixed Alperton secondary school where she carried out research faced conflicts in the form of state legislation around the curriculum influencing their ability to make professional decisions and to carry out professional actions according to their knowledge and understanding of the students they taught. For example, pressure was put on the Head of Science to convert an informal after-school Science Club he instigated into a formal, writing-focused curriculum activity for students; there was the problem of pressure to 'teach to the tests' (SATS); the issue of student learning being assessed through the written second language when students' oral skills were more highly developed and, finally, the reduction of the 100% coursework requirement from the English language GCSE to 30-40%, a requirement which had in the past served an important function as a counselling and socialising activity for students as well as a means of developing English language skills. However, in spite of the negotiation, compromise and consensus around the imposition of the official hegemonic curriculum, teachers were able to offer their students the form of 'education' and curriculum which did make connections with their lives.

In this school, teachers and students struggled to make the school curriculum their own. Instead of accepting the state-defined version, together, they re-worked it, bringing into the curriculum elements of their lives and the lives of their families.

This case study illustrates that, however comprehensive and secure statutorily defined curriculum policy appears to be, the translation of that policy into practice is not necessarily and inevitably reproductive of the values and social relationships in the way it was intended by the groups from which it originated.

CASE STUDY TWO: TRANSITION TO WORK CURRICULA IN THREE SECONDARY SCHOOLS, NEW ZEALAND

Ronald Sultana's (1989) research focused on ways in which working class students contested transition-to-work curricula in three secondary schools in New Zealand. Even though these curricula were not designated 'curricula for all' or entitlement curricula, the social reproductive intentions of the official curriculum were never totally successful as they constantly met with re-interpretation, recreation and rejection by students who were participating in them. In this case, the compulsory vocational curricula were constructed to meet the perceived needs of those students considered to be 'at risk' of unemployment (Sultana, 1989). However, students involved in the programmes contested and resisted them in a number of ways:

1. Teachers saw the programme to be concerned with personal development and giving the students the opportunities to experience different jobs in order to be better placed to make employment choices, whereas students saw the programme as an opportunity to gain work experience, to obtain good references and to make contacts with employers;

2. Teachers aimed the programme at non-academic, 'problem' students who, it was believed would find it difficult to 'survive in the world beyond school' (p 297). The research revealed that it may have been the academic, more middle class students who needed the programme most;

3. Students contested the deficit labels allocated through their participation in the programme;

4. The transition curriculum was regarded as irrelevant and inaccurate to students as it did not recognise key features of their working class youth cultures;

5. Periods of unpaid work experience with no prospects of securing employment were contested as they represented worker exploitation to students.

> Through reproduction-oriented messages
> and structures, the schools in question
> attempt to define meanings and futures for
> groups of working class students: through
> active contestation of such messages and
> structures, these students attempt to impose
> their own meanings and experiences on
> what the school has to offer (Sultana, 1989,
> p 288).

As stated, curriculum is political: mass youth unemployment triggered the need for vocational training in New Zealand at this time and transition curricula were developed to provide a link between school and work: to produce better trained workers and to allow students to have a choice of work. However, since the jobs were simply not there, and the values, perspectives and interests of the students were so far removed from those who constructed the curricula, it is hardly surprising that this high level of contestation took place.

CASE STUDY THREE: COMPREHENSIVE HIGH SCHOOL, NEW YORK, USA

Curriculum contestation in the Comprehensive High School, New York where Michelle Fine (1991) carried out her ethnographic research took the form of a drop-out rate of 40-60% amongst the school population of predominantly African-American and Latino students. She tells a story of students who have been "framed' by an institution that produces and then justifies majority failure' (P 8) by claiming to offer access to a curriculum for everyone, whilst, at the same time, producing unequal outcomes for certain social groups, namely low income, urban African-Americans and Latino youth. She describes how exclusion occurs through the absence of an appropriate curriculum for these students, exemplified by some teachers showing disrespect for students' parents;

the use of racist texts in classes; the problem of school not being able to take into account family problems at home; the silencing of students who wished to criticise the curriculum or the structures of inequality around them; the lack of opportunity for students to express their own opinions in classes and, finally, the knowledge that, even with a high school diploma, they would not find work. The extract which follows is a typical demonstration of the 'silencing' or 'smoothing over' of issues about social inequalities within the curriculum:

Field Note, October 17, Business Class

White teacher: What's EOE?

African-American male student 1: Equal over time.

White teacher: Not quite. Anyone else?

African-American female students: Equal Opportunity Employer.

White teacher: That's right.

African-American male student 2: What does that mean?

Teacher: That means that an employer can't discriminate on the basis of sex, age, marital status or race.

African-American male student 2: But wait, sometimes white people only hire white people.

Teacher: No, they're not supposed to if they say EOE in their ads. Now take out your homework.

Later that day.

MF to teacher: Why don't you discuss racism in your class?

Teacher: It would demoralise the students, they need
to feel positive and optimistic - like they have a chance.
Racism is just an excuse they use not to try harder.

(Fine, 1991, pp 36-37).

Fine demonstrates through fine grained descriptions of curricular
experiences of students in school how the complex process of
marginalisation and exclusion occurs.

ACTIVITY FIVE
Read Elliott, J. (1998) *The Curriculum Experiment:*
Meeting the Challenge of Social Change,
Buckingham: Open University Press, Chapter 3,
pp 42-57

Questions to think about
1. How much do you agree with Elliott that the
problem of disaffection ....'lies in curricular
practices - the ways in which schools organise and
transact formal learning - whose aims, purposes and
norms have failed to keep up with social change'
(p 47)?

2. What curriculum changes do Carlen et al (1992)
argue are needed to solve the problem of non
attendance at school?

CONCLUSION

How, then, does curriculum contribute towards the construction of
difference and difficulty? Moving from the one-dimensional view of
curriculum as content or syllabus, it is possible to become entwined in
much more complex, subtle and worrying ideas about what curriculum is
and what it does. The definition given on p 9 shows how academics,
given half a chance, can make something very complicated out of what
initially appears to be an unproblematical concept! The reason this

happens is because of the knowledge that curriculum plays an important part in determining how socially just an educational system may be.

If curriculum constructors and curriculum developers do not acknowledge its power as a political tool, if they do not appreciate that curriculum knowledge may make connections only with a limited number of students, and not with all, then curriculum will continue to operate as an unequal and socially unjust process. It will continue to deny the experience of education to all by constructing some groups of students as 'different' from 'the norm' and by marginalising them from the experience of education, to create for them educational difficulty. It will continue to privilege certain groups by making connections with their cultural backgrounds, celebrating their forms of knowledge, ideas and cultural practices which have been dominant in social life.

In this unit you have looked at a wide range of ideas concerning curriculum. I hope that these ideas have helped you to think critically about the curriculum with which you work.

REFERENCES

Apple, M. J. (1996) *Cultural Politics and Education,* Buckingham: Open University Press

Armstrong, F. (1999a) 'Inclusion, Curriculum and the Struggle for Space In School' in *The International Journal on Inclusive Education* (forthcoming).

Armstrong, F. (1999b) 'The Curriculum as Alchemy: School and the Struggle for Cultural Space' in *Curriculum Studies,* Vol 3, No 1.

Ball, S.J. (1990) *Foucault and Education*, London: Routledge

Blenkin, G.M., Edwards, G. and Kelly, A.V. (1992) *Change and the Curriculum*, London: Paul Chapman

Blumer, H. (1969) *Symbolic Interactionism: Perspective and Method*, Englewood Cliffs, New Jersey: Prentice Hall Inc.

Blumer, H. (1971) 'Sociological Implications of the thought of George Herbert Mead' in Cosin, B.R., Dale, I.R., Esland,G.M., Mackinnon, D. and Swift, D.F. *School and Society: A Sociological Reader*, London: Routledge and Kegan Paul

Carr, W. and Hartnett, A. (1996) *Education and the Struggle for Democracy*, Buckingham: Open University Press

Chessum, M. (1980) 'Teacher Ideologies and Pupil Disaffection' in Barton, L., Meighan, R. and Walker, S. *Schooling, Ideology and the Curriculum*, Lewes: Falmer

Department for Education (DfE) (1995) *The National Curriculum*, London: HMSO

Elliott, J. (1998) *The Curriculum Experiment: Meeting the Challenge of Social Change*, Buckingham: Open University Press

Fine, M. (1991) *Framing Dropouts: Notes on the Politics of an Urban Public High School*, Albany: State University of New York

204

Foucault, M. (1972) *The Archaeology of Knowledge,* London: Tavistock Publications

Gramsci, A. (1971) *Selections from the Prison Notebooks* (edited and translated by Quentin Hoare and Geoffrey Nowell Smith) New York: International Publishers

Green, A. (1990) *Education and State Formation,* New York: St Martin's Press

Hall, S. (1981) 'Schooling, State and Society' in Dale, R., Esland, G., Ferguson, R., and MacDonald, M., *Education and the State,* Falmer and Open University Press

Hamilton, D. (1990) *Learning about Education: An Unfinished Curriculum,* Milton Keynes: Open University Press

Kelly, A. V. (1990) *The National Curriculum: A Critical Review,* London: Paul Chapman

Mead, G. H. (1934) *Mind, Self and Society,* Chicago: Chicago University Press

Riseborough, G. (1985) 'Pupils, Teachers' Careers and Schooling: an Empirical Study' in Ball, S.J. and Goodson, I.F. *Teachers' Lives and Careers,* Lewes, East Sussex: Falmer

Robinson, K. (1992) 'Classroom Discipline: power, resistance and gender. A look at teacher perspectives' in *Gender and Education*, Vol 4, No 3, pp 273 - 287

Stenhouse, L. (1975) *An Introduction to Curriculum Research and Development*, London: Heineman

Sultana, R. G. (1989) 'Transition Education, Student Contestation and the production of Meaning: Possibilities and Limitations of Resistance Theories' in *British Journal of Sociology of Education*, Vol 10, No 3, pp 287 - 309

Usher, R. and Edwards, R. (1994) *Postmodernism and Education*, London: Routledge

Whitty, G., Power, S. and Halpin, D. (1998) *Devolution and Choice in Education*, Buckingham: Open University Press

Winter, C. (1997) 'Teacher Professionalism and the Changing Discourse of the Humanities Curriculum' in *Teacher Development*, Vol 1, No 2, pp 191 - 204

UNIT EIGHT

IDENTITY, DIFFERENCE AND CURRICULUM: A CASE STUDY IN CULTURAL POLITICS

ROGER SLEE

INTRODUCTION

Ambitious in scope, this unit aims to explore a number of issues summoned by mention of *inclusive schooling* and *curriculum* in the same breath. In doing so, I will raise a number of key questions about the constitution of the invention of mass compulsory schooling as we know it and about the most fundamental question of all: who are schools for? Answering this question may then encourage us to move on to pose a follow-up question: what should they teach? The unit will invite the reader to consider clues, blatant and subtle, provided by the curriculum to help us answer the first question. My initial response is that schools were never meant for everyone, and notwithstanding recent policy narratives of inclusion, the school gate still stands as an electronic turnstile which bars entry to those children who do not metaphorically hold the correct pin-number.

The unit is organised into three sections. Section One: A Stipulative Language, encourages students to lay bare the epistemological foundations for their understanding of disability, difference and inclusion. This is done prior to Section Two: Curriculum as Cultural Metaphor, on the understanding that varying forms of knowledge about disability will produce different curricular options. Section Three: The

Inclusive School, draws upon a number of observations from the field to establish some preconditions for more inclusive curriculum.

I hasten to add that the final section is not an educational DIY, a paint-by-numbers approach to inclusion. What is manifest in this brief unit is the degree of discontinuity of policy between centre and locality, fragmentation within and between schools. Therefore, broad brush prescriptions for 'doing inclusion' emanating from reform movements such as school effectiveness research and the school improvement movement have fundamental flaws and may in fact contribute further to the exclusion of disabled students (Slee, 1998).

The reader will also notice that the activities in the unit are simply offered as prompts to further reading, discussion and debate. Our work in this area is ongoing. This unit hopes to provide some prompts and options for your continuing inquiries into the processes of educational exclusion and inclusion with particular reference to the articulation of disability and education.

SECTION ONE: A STIPULATIVE LANGUAGE.

Consider the following extract from Joseph P. Shapiro's (1993) carefully titled text on disability politics in the USA, *No Pity*:

> Nondisabled Americans do not understand disabled ones
>
> That was clear at the memorial service for Timothy Cook, when long-time friends got up to pay him heartfelt tribute. "He never seemed disabled to me," said one. "He was the least disabled person I ever met," pronounced another. It was the highest praise these nondisabled friends could think to give a disabled attorney who, at thirty-eight years old, had won land-mark disability rights cases, including one to force public transit systems to equip their buses with wheelchair lifts. But more than a few heads in the crowded chapel bowed with an uneasy embarrassment at the supposed compliment. It was as if someone had tried to compliment a black man by saying, "You're the least black person I ever met," as false as telling a Jew, "I never think of you as Jewish," as clumsy as seeking to flatter a woman with "You don't act like a woman."
>
> Here in this memorial chapel was a small clash between the reality of disabled people and the understanding of their lives by others. It was the type of collision that disabled people experience daily. Yet any discordancy went unnoticed even to the well-meaning friends of a disability rights fighter like Cook.
>
> (Shapiro, 1993: 3 – 4)

Shapiro's point is clear and powerful. Using the same general linguistic framework, say English or Spanish or Mandarin Chinese, is no guarantee for shared meanings. How we come to know about phenomena shapes our understanding of it, and in turn, frames the meanings we ascribe to that phenomena when speaking about or acting on it. Put simply, I can use the same vocabulary as you to describe something. However, the meaning that I want to establish for my statements may be very much at odds with your interpretation. The meanings you attach to the vocabulary that I use come from a totally different world. There is an epistemological problem. Returning to Joseph Shapiro's general observation – nondisabled Americans do not understand disabled Americans. We may press this further to suggest that within each of these broad defining categories, disabled and nondisabled, there exists a constellation of varied and contested understandings. Moreover, the views do not necessarily constitute themselves according to the convenient categories of nondisabled and disabled.

Let me explain this further. At a conference dealing with progress towards what was then referred to as the 'integration' of disabled students into regular schools and classrooms in Australia, the delegates came from the different states and territories within the continent. In conversation over coffee before the commencement of the conference proceedings and in break times they would chat, apparently comfortably, about 'integration' with each other. As each of the state and territory education authority officials took to the podium to describe their department's initiatives it was clear that they spoke of very different things but used a common vocabulary to describe it. For one state integration was the partial involvement of disabled students in the social activities of the neighbouring regular school followed by their return to the segregated special school. For another, it was the establishment of the right of all children to enrol in their neighbourhood school. And for still another, integration represented the targeting of a particular group of disabled students, say wheelchair users or deaf students, and bringing them into the regular classroom. Intellectually disabled [learning difficulties as it is described elsewhere] would be phase two of integration policy. From this point onwards coffee breaks became more difficult as people stipulated their meanings and engaged in debate about the meanings of their language.

The choice becomes plain. Do we pretend agreement or do we, as Peter Clough and Len Barton (1995) encourage us to do, acknowledge the political and educational necessity of *making difficulties*? This section is about the difficult debates that must be had. It is about stipulating our meanings for disability, disablement, exclusion and inclusion. The two questions set for us here are:

- *What is disability?*
- *What is inclusive education?*

Another question lurks behind these two to assist with our answers:

- *How did we arrive at these answers?*

I will argue as others before me (Abberley, 1987; Barton, 1987; Oliver, 1990; Barnes, 1990; Morris, 1991) that there is a too frequently ignored politics to making meaning when it comes to disability. We will return to this point shortly to establish disablement as a form of oppression. This will have fundamental implications for curriculum and for our notions of inclusive education.

UNDERSTANDING DISABLEMENT

How do we come to learn about and know disability? For most us the answer is, 'from a distance' and through the powerful discourses of knowledgeable others. Discursive practices establish the frames within which we will piece together our understandings. For Foucault (1997:11) discursive practices are:

> ...characterised by the demarcation of a field of objects, by the definition of a legitimate perspective for a subject of knowledge, by the setting of norms for elaborating concepts and theories. Hence each of them presupposes a play of prescriptions that govern exclusions and selections.... A discursive practice brings together various disciplines or sciences, or it passes through a number of them and gathers several of their areas into a sometimes inconspicuous cluster.

Discursive practices have constructed the category, official knowledge and treatment of the 'special educational needs' [SEN] student. This discourse of special educational needs has become a very powerful knowledge (Usher, 1998) which draws together and is used to map, regulate and govern (Rose, 1989) a fragmented and unruly population of 'different others' with less than *docile bodies'* (Foucault, 1977).

Discourse is used in this unit to refer not just to language stated or written, it is used to refer to fields of language and action which establishes the framework for meaning and understanding. Mike Oliver referred to this in a discussion with Master of Education students at Goldsmiths College University of London in 1996 as 'disability stories' which represent alternative models of disability. These models have direct and profound impacts upon policy choices and upon who does the choosing. Let us briefly rehearse some of these stories which Oliver (1996) has conveniently framed within a table showing alternative models for understanding disability by examining our own epistemological formations.

Disability Models

The individual model	*The social model*
personal tragedy theory	*social oppression theory*
personal problem	*social problem*
individual treatment	*social action*
medicalisation	*self-help*
professional dominance	*individual and collective responsibility*
expertise	*experience*
adjustment	*collective identity*
individual identity	*collective identity*
prejudice	*discrimination*
attitudes	*behaviour*
care	*rights*
control	*choice*
policy	*politics*
individual adaptation	*social change*

(Oliver, 1996:34)

Exploring my own biography I have to report with considerable shame a set of notions about disabled people which Michael Oliver would consign to disability as 'personal tragedy' stories. For my school friends and me, 'special kids' were sent to special schools [sic. segregated schools] because unfortunately they weren't 'normal'. The sociological definition of normality for the primary school kid? 'Not like us'. Nature had been unkind and they couldn't mix with us, as they couldn't learn as much. What they did learn took a longer time so they had specially trained, and very caring, teachers to look after them. Their education was after all very much an exercise in care. We never saw them – except some went to the shops with their parents, but many didn't do that either.

Etiological explanations were extracted from my parents who usually summoned confounding medical terminology and advised sympathetic attitude, 'For there but for the grace of God, go I'. Our school teachers also read stories to reinforce our pity for disabled people, to underline the need for kindly disposition mixed with stories of the heroic disabled like Helen Keller or Douglas Bader; we had no special Olympics! Prior to starting primary school I remember that I would accompany my mother as she did her part time job of cleaning the houses of wealthy people in the town. She did this with a woman who had a daughter who, I was told, was mongoloid – I forget the girl's name, but I do remember this harsh term. One morning we went to their house. The curtains were drawn, the mother was in her dressing gown and her daughter wasn't there. My mother embraced her sobbing friend. I didn't understand what was happening but sufficiently comprehended the portents of calamity to render myself invisible. On the way home I interrogated my mother to find that the daughter had been electrocuted in her bath the previous day – it was *sad but also a blessing*. I learned that death was better than a disabled life.

Memory suggests that my education about disability was suspended until my teacher education programme. It reinforced some of the early learning, but drew on far more sophisticated discourse to do so. Special education was a separate discipline that seemed to call on a very technical range of psychological, statistical and medical foundations. My education had some predictable outcomes. I felt embarrassed in the company of disabled children – I didn't know what to do. The logical was simple: had I done special education I would know what to do. I firmly believed that the education of some children was not the business of my classroom. My answer to the first question was formed - schooling was for 'normal' kids.

This miseducation was shaken when in my first teaching appointment I was told that 'Brendan', a blind boy, was in my Year 12 Politics class. I was anxious and it may have revealed itself as I raised my voice to address the startled lad. His classmates were not so inept. Brendan had been the victim of a prank at the school gone terribly wrong. His classmates knew him and knew that the only difference was that Brendan couldn't see anymore and that he got mad and depressed about that. They also learnt what to do to help him. These kids saw to it that Brendan's learning didn't suffer while I was learning how to be his teacher and unlearning my established understandings of disability and special needs.

My re-education commenced in earnest when I took a teaching position in a Teaching Unit [Behaviour Unit] for so-called 'at risk students'. What I have subsequently read about this kind of educational provision (HMI, 1978; Mongon, 1988) quickly became apparent to me and set up an epistemological tension. I had decided that if I was going to be able to help these kids who came to the unit, I needed a Graduate Diploma in Special Education. I would then be able to diagnose their needs and draw from or create the correct programme for remediation. At the same time it seemed that schools were a key feature of the risk for these young people. More precisely the schools didn't really want them back after their time at the unit. This was made plain by institutional inflexibility and the assumption that the kids would learn how to comply with the punitive culture of schools as they experienced it, overcome years of failure in the space of a school term, and then become successful model students. What also worried me was the growing number of units holding onto an increasing population of children destined never to return to the regular school. There was an implicit commissioning of schools to remain the same despite the changing character and needs of their student cohorts.

The fundamental change in my understanding of disablement came in the form of a different research literature suggested by Bob Semmens, a lonely criminologist in a special education faculty. Through his tutelage I read Sally Tomlinson's (1981, 1982) sociological study of special education and Caribbean students in the UK; to consider the implications of Len Barton's (1987) pronouncement that special educational needs was a euphemism for the failure of schools; and his sponsorship of disabled researchers and activists in the sociology of special education.

Looking back at Michael Oliver's table of individual and social models of disability, I can now delineate key moments in my understanding which draw elements from both. As a child I was immersed in a 'common knowledge' of disability as a descriptor of defective individual pathology. Medical explanations were sought and provided to explain what was considered abnormal. Educational responses to disability operated according to an individual medical model of treatment and service delivery. The expertise of professionals (Skrtic, 1991; Tomlinson, 1996) was privileged over the collective experience of disabled students, their parents or advocates. Children were segregated for this intervention which was 'in their best interest' (Walsh, 1993). Where once a personal tragedy and sympathy discourse dominated the field, the discourse has become increasingly technical and bureaucratic (Fulcher, 1989).

Special educational has moved into the regular school as well as maintaining its traditional site and donning the linguistic garments of inclusive education is still treating individuals through highly technical processes of diagnosis and the deployment of additional resources and programmes grafted onto the educational mainstream. Disability remains a problem to be fixed through inclusive educational policies (Branson and Miller, 1989). The disabled child is still seen as dysfunctional, as the locus of a problem for mass schooling to have to deal with.

The social model of disablement (Oliver, 1990, 1996) draws on 'the sociological imagination' (Wright Mills, 1959) to distinguish between personal troubles and social issues. Disablement refers to a deep structure of oppression; it is not a medical condition or a symptom of uncharitable attitudes. Impairment, as Abberley (1987) asserts, is historically and culturally specific signifying changes in the material conditions of production, the advances of medical technology and the specificity of lifestyles. According to this scenario remedial action is misdirected in its application to individuals.

This has specific implications for school curriculum. When talking about inclusive education we need to hold onto our knowledge of disability as our point of commencement. Following the Activity 1 we will attempt to frame an approach to stipulating 'inclusive education'.

> **ACTIVITY ONE**
> **You are invited to consider your own acquisition of knowledge about disability. Carefully read the following readings:**
>
> **Oliver, M. (1996) *Understanding Disability. From Theory to Practice*, London, Macmillan. (Chapters 2 & 3)**
>
> **Fulcher, G. (1989) *Disabling Policies?* Lewes, Falmer Press. (Chapter 1)**
>
> **Considering the key moments in your discovery of knowledge about disability, what discourses have shaped that knowledge and how has it changed over the years?**

EDUCATIONAL DISABLEMENT AND INCLUSIVE SCHOOLING.

At the heart of this explication of inclusive schooling is a rejection of the relocation of special education as the foundation for a more inclusive education. Such a position is reductionist and fails to acknowledge the relationship of school to the process of disablement or the interest of professions in maintaining traditional knowledge about disability. Location is not the issue here; the critical issue concerns the politics of segregation and choice. Without a careful analysis of the pervasive oppression of disabled students through the deep structure and culture of various forms of education, recent analyses of inclusive and special education (Jenkinson, 1997; Clark, Dyson, Millward and Skidmore, 1997) fail to engage in the project of cultural politics which is demanded. Greater individualisation of programmes, the provision of a more expansive range of options for the placement of students, increases in resources and personnel are not of themselves the requirements for inclusive schooling.

Tony Booth (1995) urges that we problematise the notion of inclusion, acknowledge the taboo of the politics of education and predicate our understanding of inclusion with a clear comprehension of educational exclusion. Consistent with our discussion of disablement as a social process, this analysis leads us to look not just at the differences of the child for explanation of disjuncture and disfunctionality, it invites us to consider the complex relationships between forms of educational practice and children. Inclusive schooling is not about additional programmes grafted onto schools or provided at the margins. Nor is inclusive schooling about the changing form of special educational provision and the guarantee of special educational studies in basic teacher training programmes.

Inclusive schooling is better understood in terms of the investigation into and the reconstruction of the pathologies of both regular and special educational provision (Slee, 1996). Questions about the degree to which schooling embraces the politics of recognition become apposite. To what extent is disability framed within the educational reform politics of anti-racist, gender equity and socio-economic class based disadvantage and exclusion? Inclusion is not about the discursive practices of individual psycho-medical models of special educational needs; it is a form of cultural politics. The quest is not to assimilate different kids and minimise institutional disequilibrium, it moves into the field of human rights (Barton, 1997).

SECTION TWO: CURRICULUM AS CULTURAL METAPHOR

WHAT IS CURRICULUM?

The simple answer to this direct question is everything that goes on at school. It is not just about the formal syllabus and programme of instruction advertised in the school prospectus. Nor is it just about the intended outcomes from the National Curriculum such as that promulgated by the Education Reform Act (1988) in the United Kingdom. Preston and Symes (1992) put it this way:

> We have argued that curriculum is a scaled down version of culture, a selection in miniature of the highlights of Western civilisation, or at least those which a powerful minority has deemed to be such. ... there has always been considerable debate about how this model of Western thought should be organised and shaped, and what within it should be given greatest emphasis and force (this is often phrased as the 'knowledge most worth having').
> (Preston & Symes, 1993: 84 – 85)

Children learn many other lessons that are not expressed in the formal curriculum. Sometimes referred to as the 'hidden curriculum' this provides space for expansive cultural learning. Choices about subjects to be included in the curriculum axiomatically produces a null curriculum; that which is excluded and consequently devalued.

The Australian History syllabus taught to Year Nine students across Australia for many years commenced with the early European explorers and the intrepid adventures of a sailor from Yorkshire named Cook as he, and later Arthur Phillip battled against the 'savages' who inhabited this 'empty continent'. Aboriginal history and culture was thus expunged by this official knowledge (Apple, 1993). In similar fashion, history never gave 'her story'. Students, girls and boys, studied about men as they shaped ideas, made scientific and geographic discoveries, and created the artistic and political culture of a developing nation. Many 'Australian' students found that their cultural, racial and social identities were bleached out of the syllabus on offer. They read of a world, across all of their school subjects, which denied their existence. Students from non-English speaking backgrounds, working class students, girls, disabled students, geographically isolated and indigenous students were disadvantaged by a syllabus that failed to include their identity in anything other than disparaging forms in its account of the world. Inclusive schooling is thus about bringing these students back into the centre of school life – it is about the articulation of their worlds within the curriculum.

The subjects taught tell students whom schools are for. If we trace the development of the curriculum we can note the absences.

Stephen Ball (1994) reflects on the current National Curriculum in the UK as 'curriculum as museum', 'the curriculum of the dead'. His analysis of cultural restorationism within the music syllabus is worth noting:

> Music is defined solely in terms of product, in terms of what others, listed in the canon, do. For the restorationists music is not a putting together of sounds to create effect or shared activity, it is not a matter of creativity, but rather a lonely appreciation, a fossilised tradition, a mental abstraction divorced from the here

> and now and from the possibility of
> engagement. Education and learning here
> are founded upon alienation, a negation of
> self; knowledge is valued precisely for its
> irrelevance, esotericism, detachment,
> elitism and intrinsic difficulty; learning is
> an act of abasement, of passivity, of
> deference. The learner comes to the
> knowledge naïve and innocent and leaves
> that which is learned untouched and
> unchanged.
>
> (Ball, 1994:35)

It is clear in this account that pedagogy is also an important aspect of the process of educational marginalisation or exclusion. How students are taught has the capacity to engage or disengage, the capacity to reveal or conceal knowledge, the capacity to enable students to learn or to disable them. Failure is not solely representative of students' capacity to learn, it reflects a much more complex pathology of schooling. Special needs may reflect limitations in the imagination of curriculum developers and the teaching repertoire of teachers. It may represent, as Corbett (1998) observes, the unequal entitlement of educational provision.

Within the general area of pedagogy there are a range of aspects worth considering as agents for inclusive practice or exclusion. Styles of teaching that are teacher centred are advanced by proponents of school effectiveness research (Reynolds and Farrell, 1996) as a model for the successful school. This has been very influential in the shaping of the National Curriculum for Teacher Training. However, others such as Robert Slavin and his colleagues (1989) and Mehan et al (1996) argue the case for support for the spectrum of teaching and learning styles to cater for all students. Approaches to assessment may be norm referenced or criterion referenced (Black, 1998; Gipps, 1994). Testing may act as a summative pronouncement of failure and be non-redemptive or it may be applied as a progressive assessment schedule to establish progress and design steps for its continuation.

The organisation of schooling is also a structural feature of educational exclusion and inclusion. Readers may wish to explore this with reference to the intricate detail of a school's operating procedures and organisational features. I will select one aspect of the organisation of schooling that has contributed to more exclusionary forms of schooling: the marketisation of schooling. Gewirtz, Ball and Bowe (1995) have drawn on an abundant qualitative data to demonstrate the way in which the creation of educational markets reinforces existing cultural and social advantages of well-resourced choosers. 'Class selection', they declare, 'is revalorized by the market' (Gewirtz, all and Bowe, 1995:23). Earlier work (Gold, Bowe and Ball, 1993; Barton and Landman, 1993) identified the vulnerability of disabled students in a market where schools derived their competitive edge from the published performance outcomes of students in GCSE examinations.

CURRICULUM VALUES?

A subtext of the preceding discussion is the role of the values articulated through the curriculum. In other words, what message is derived from the content of learning, from the approaches to teaching, from the organisation of schools and the ethos that they embrace? It may be appropriate to reflect upon other excluded groups of students to frame an agenda for a 'pedagogy of recognition' (Nixon et al, 1997).

ACTIVITY TWO

Consider the strategies adopted by feminist and anti racist educators and educational researchers who sought to address the deleterious impacts of sexism and racism in schooling? You will note that the readings apply C. Wright Mills (1959) 'Sociological Imagination' to establish the problems of sexism and racism in education as structural social issues and not individualised personal troubles. Accordingly models of individual intervention or compensatory programmes are not useful to the task of producing an enabling education through the elimination of sexism and racism.

Read the following:
Troyna, B. (1993) *Racism and Education*, Buckingham, Open University Press.
[Critical Introduction by Fazal Rizvi;
Chapters 4 & 7]

Weiner, G. (1994) *Feminisms in Education*, Buckingham, Open University Press.
[Chapters 5 & 6]

Consider the following questions in relation to what you have read.

Were their questions concerned with locating failure in their constituencies?

Did they seek compensatory programmes to offset the structural problems they encountered in schools?

What did they target in promoting change?

Your reading and discussion for Activity 2 may have led you to examine the cultural politics of gender and education. You may have determined that the problem was not girls, but patriarchy. The recognition of this political struggle suggests a need to confront patriarchy as it is articulated through the curriculum, through pedagogy, and through the organisation and ethos of schooling. Likewise for racism (Troyna, 1993; Gillborn, 1995; Sewell, 1997).

SECTION THREE: THE INCLUSIVE SCHOOL.

In this final section of the unit I will simply make a series of points which are designed to guide your reading, thinking and discussions about the potential for inclusive schooling. The points will proceed from the key issues laid out in sections 1 and 2 of this unit.

THE POLITICS OF RECOGNITION.

Becky Walsh (1993), while still a student teacher, wrote about her experiences of special education and suggested that what was done 'in her best interest' often limited her opportunities outside the special school. Her educational battle was a struggle to overcome a narrow and limiting curriculum. The expert knowledge of professional workers in the field of special educational needs stood between her and her potential. Disabled researchers are stating their pride in their identity and struggling to assert their voice in the reconstitution of their schooling (Morris, 1991; Oliver, 1996; Campbell and Oliver, 1996).

Voice is a critical element in the struggle of all marginalised people. Inclusive schooling is not simply about the special educational industry becoming ventriloquists through assuming an inclusive discourse. A new kind of listening has to be effected. Inclusion is not simply about bureaucratic/technical policy solutions for the 'problem' of disability (Fulcher, 1989; Branson and Miller, 1989). Disablement is a reflection of oppressive discursive practices. A politics of recognition presents an alternative to individual medical discourses of disability and interrupts the current disposition towards distributive solutions within the existing organisational framework (Slee, 1996; Rizvi and Lingard, 1996).

> **ACTIVITY THREE**
> **Read the following:**
> Slee, R. (1996) 'Inclusive Education in Australia? Not Yet!', *Cambridge Journal of Education*, Vol. 26, No. 1: 19 – 32.
>
> Corbett, J. (1997)'Include/exclude: redefining the boundaries', *International Journal of Inclusive Education*, Vol. 1, No. 1: 55 – 64.
>
> Barton, L. (1997) 'Inclusive education: romantic, subversive or realistic?', *International Journal of Inclusive Education*, Vol. 1, No. 3: 231 – 242.
>
> Inclusive schooling like other aspects of education policy is a site of contestation. Outline the tensions within and between the above papers. In your notes, consider your own position in relation to them.

SITES FOR ACTION.

The wisdom of grand policy prescriptions devised at centre and delivered locally has been robustly challenged (Ball, 1994; Slee, 1995; Taylor, Rizvi, Lingard and Henry, 1997; Whitty, Power and Halpin, 1998) in the field of education policy studies. The challenge is to establish broad educational principles that enable local action to develop collaborative communities. Local specificity ought to be encouraged within classrooms and school communities consistent with a broader framework that recognises diversity. This is not apologia for a liberal 'have a nice day' soup of tokenism (hooks, 1994). hooks (1994:31) quotes Peter MacLaren to emphasise her point:

> Diversity that somehow constitutes itself as a harmonious ensemble of benign cultural spheres is a conservative and liberal model of multiculturalism that, in my mind, deserves to be jettisoned because, when we try to make culture an undisturbed space of harmony and agreement where social relations exist within cultural forms of uninterrupted accords we subscribe to a form of social amnesia in which we forget that all knowledge is forged in histories that are played out in the field of social antagonisms.
> (Peter MacLaren quoted in hooks, 1994:31)

Barton warns against political cul-de-sacs in liberal and post-modern theorising (Barton, 1997: 240). While academically acceptable, he contends that they threaten to undermine the development of 'an adequate theory of political agency' pursuant to the project of inclusive education.

IMAGINATION AND RECONSTRUCTION

Though it may not be currently fashionable in education theory the point of departure for this unit in inclusive curriculum is an invitation to reconsider the dialogues of a couple of critical theorists – Paulo Friere and Ira Shor (1987). Ira tells Paulo of the imagination that is required 'where students and teachers practice anticipating a new social reality'. He elaborates:

> Imagination can be exercised as a resource to expel dominant ideology and to open up some space in consciousness for transcending thinking. I've asked students to be imaginative generally in courses I teach. Our social inquiries regularly include a moment called "reconstruction",

> where I ask students to imagine alternatives
> to the social problem they have
> investigated, as a model of future solutions.
> (Friere and Shor, 1987: 185)

This call to 'think otherwise' (Ball, 1995) is a sound practice for educators. This unit invites you to engage in a 'moment of reconstruction' to imagine an inclusive curriculum. Your imagination will, I contend, be greatly assisted by reference to the voice of disabled researchers in this act of critical engagement with the possibilities of an inclusive curriculum.

REFERENCES

Abberley, P. (1987) 'The concept of oppression and the development of a social theory of disability' in *Disability, Handicap & Society*, Vol 2, No 1, pp 5 – 19.

Apple, M. (1993) *Official Knowledge: Democratic Education in a Conservative Age*, New York: Routledge.

Ball, S. J. (1994) *Education Reform: A Critical and Post-structural Approach*, Buckingham: Open University Press.

Ball, S.J. (1995) 'Intellectuals or Technicians? The urgent role of theory in educational studies' in *British Journal of Educational Studies*, Vol 43, No 3, pp 255 – 271.

Barnes, C. (1990) *Cabbage Syndrome: The Social Construction of Dependency*, London: Falmer Press.

Barton, L. (Ed) (1987) *The Politics of Special Educational Needs*, Lewes: Falmer Press.

Barton, L. (Ed) (1996) *Disability and Society: Emerging Issues and Insights*, Harlow: Addison Wesley Longman.

Barton, L. (1997) 'Inclusive Education: romantic, subversive or realistic?' in *International Journal of Inclusive Education*, Vol 1, No 3, pp 231 – 242.

Barton, L. and Landman, M. (1993) 'The Politics of Integration: Observations on the Warnock Report' in Slee, R. (Ed) *Is There A Desk With My Name On It? The Politics of Integration*, London: Falmer Press.

Black, P. (1998) *Testing: Friend or Foe? Theory and Practice of Assessment and Testing*, London: Falmer Press.

Booth, T. (1995) 'The poverty of special education: theories to the rescue?' in Clark, C., Dyson, A. and Millward, A. (Eds) *Theorising Special Education*, London: Routledge.

Branson, J. and Miller, D. (1989) 'Beyond Integration Policy – the Deconstruction of Disability' in Barton, L. (Ed) *Integration: Myth or Reality?*, Lewes: Falmer Press.

Campbell, J. and Oliver, M. (1996) *Disability Politics. Understanding Our Past, Changing Our Future*, London: Routledge.

Clark, C., Dyson, A., Millward, A. and Skidmore, D. (1997) *New Directions in Special Needs. Innovations in Mainstream Schools*, London: Cassell.

Clough, P. and Barton, L. (Eds.) (1995) *Making Difficulties: Research and the Construction of SEN*, London: Paul Chapman Publishing.

Corbett, J. (1995) *Bad-Mouthing: The Language of Special Needs*, London: Falmer Press.

Corbett, J. (1997) 'Include/exclude: redefining the boundaries' in *International Journal of Inclusive Education*, Vol 1, No 1, pp 55 – 64.

Corbett, J. (1998) *Special Educational Needs in the Twentieth Century. A Cultural Analysis*, London: Cassell.

Foucault, M. (1977) *Discipline and Punish: The Birth of the Prison*, London: Allen Lane.

Foucault, M. (1997) **Ethics. The Essential Works 1**, (Edited by Paul Rabinow), London, Allen Lane: The Penguin Press.

Friere, P. and Shor, I. (1987) *A Pedagogy for Liberation. Dialogues on Transforming Education*, Basingstoke: Macmillan.

Fulcher, G. (1989) *Disabling Policies?*, Lewes: Falmer Press.

Gewirtz, S., Ball, S.J. and Bowe, R. (1995) *Markets, Choice and Equity in Education*, Buckingham: Open University Press.

Gold, A., Bowe, R. and Ball, S.J. (1993) 'Special Educational Needs in a New Context: Micropolitics, Money and Education for All' in Slee, R. (Ed) *Is There A Desk With My Name On It? The Politics of Integration*, London: Falmer Press.

Gillborn, D. (1995) *Racism and Antiracism in Real Schools*, Buckingham: Open University Press.

Gipps, C. (1994) *Beyond Testing. Towards a Theory of Educational Assessment*, London: Falmer Press.

Her Majesty's Inspectorate (1978) *Behaviour Units: A Survey of Special Units for Pupils with Behavioural Problems*, London: Department of Education and Science.

hooks, b. (1994) *Teaching to Transgress. Education as the Practice of Freedom*, New York: Routledge.

Jenkinson, J.C. (1997) *Mainstream or Special? Educating Students with Disabilities*, London: Routledge.

Mehan, H., Villanneva, I., Hubbard, L. and Lintz, A. (1996) *Constructing School Success: The Consequences of Untracking Low-achieving Students*, New York: Cambridge University Press.

Mongon, D. (1988) 'Behaviour Units, *Maladjustment* and Student Control' in Slee, R. (Ed) *Discipline and Schools: A Curriculum Perspective*, Melbourne: Macmillan.

Morris, J. (1990) *Pride Against Prejudice*, London: Women's Press.

Nixon, J., Martin, J., McKeown, P. and Ranson, S. (1997) 'Confronting 'Failure': towards a pedagogy of recognition' in *International Journal of Inclusive Education*, Vol 1, No 2, pp 121 – 141.

Oliver. M. (1990) *The Politics of Disablement*, London, Macmillan.

Oliver, M. (1996) *Understanding Disability. From Theory to Practice*, London, Macmillan.

Preston, N. and Symes, C. (1992) *Schools and Classrooms. A Cultural Studies Analysis of Education*, Melbourne: Longman Cheshire.

Reynolds, D. (1995) 'Using school effectiveness knowledge for children with special needs: the problems and possibilities' in Clarke, C., Dyson, A. and Millward, A. (Eds) *Towards Inclusive Schools?* London: David Fulton.

Reynolds, D. and Farrell, S. (1996) *Worlds Apart? A Review of International Surveys of Educational Achievement Involving England*, London: HMSO.

Rose, N. (1989) *Governing The Soul*, London: Routledge.

Sewell, T. (1997) *Black Masculinities and Schooling. How Black Boys Survive Modern Schooling*, Stoke-on-Trent: Trentham Books.

Shapiro, J.P. (1993) *No Pity. People with Disabilities Forging a New Civil Rights Movement*, New York: Random House.

Skrtic, T. (1991) *Behind Special Education: A Critical Analysis of Professional Culture and School Organisation*, Denver: Love Publishing.

Slavin, R. (Ed.) (1989) *School and Classroom Organisation*, Hillsdale N.J.: Erlbaum.

Slee, R. (1995) *Changing Theories and Practices of Discipline*, London: Falmer Press.

Slee, R. (1996) 'Inclusive Education in Australia? Not Yet!' in *Cambridge Journal of Education*, Vol 26, No 1, pp 19 – 32.

Slee, R. (1998) 'High Reliability Organisations and Liability Students – the politics of recognition' in Slee, R., Weiner, G. and Tomlinson, S. (Eds) *School Effectiveness For Whom?* London: Falmer Press.

Taylor, S., Rizvi, F., Henry, M. and Lingard, B. (1997) *Educational Policy and the Politics of Change*, London: Routledge.

Tomlinson, S. (1981) *Educational Subnormality: A Study in Decision-Making*, London: Routledge and Kegan Paul.

Tomlinson, S. (1982) *A Sociology of Special Education*, London: Routledge and Kegan Paul.

Tomlinson, S. (1996) 'Conflicts and Dilemmas for Professionals in Special Education' in Christensen, C. and Rizvi, F. (Eds) *Disability and the Dilemmas of Education and Social Justice*, Buckingham: Open University Press.

Troyna, B. (1993) *Racism and Education*, Buckingham: Open University Press.

Usher, R. (1998) 'Seductive Texts: Competence, Power and Knowledge in Postmodernity' in Barnett, R. and Griffin, A. (Eds) *The End of Knowledge in Higher Education*, London: Cassell.

Walsh, B. (1993) 'How Disabling Any Handicap Is Depends on the Attitudes and Actions of Others: A Student's Perspective' in Slee, R. (Ed) *Is There A Desk With My Name On It? The Politics of Integration*, London: Falmer Press.

Weiner, G. (1994) *Feminisms in Education*, Buckingham: Open University Press.

Whitty, G., Power, S. and Halpin, D. (1998) *Devolution and Choice in Education. The School, the State and the Market*, Buckingham: Open University Press.

Wright Mills, C. (1959) *The Sociological Imagination*, New York: Oxford University Press.

UNIT NINE

INSIDER PERSPECTIVES AND PRACTITIONER RESEARCH

PETER CLOUGH

In the context of inclusive education, this Study Unit has three main aims:

- to outline some issues in the contemporary debate over research processes and effects;
- to characterise a 'research attitude' to both professional practice and academic study;
- to present some preparation for your own research activities.

INTRODUCTION: A *REAL* RESEARCH EXPERIENCE?

In 1997 I had the opportunity to speak at a colloquium with colleagues from various European states about teacher education in the area of Special Educational Needs. It was a useful experience, not least because it made me think hard and afresh about what we do in England and Wales. For the most part, I - like the majority of practitioners - go along thinking I'm doing a reasonably good job; fairly secure in the traditions of practice which define my job; to be sure, making sometimes horrendous mistakes but - for all that - nonetheless safe within the structures of my own profession.

But having to present something of what I do for a living to other people (and, particularly, a non-UK audience) made me think hard about a lot of things: about what is distinctive about 'Special' and 'Inclusive'[2] education practices in the UK; about the policy contexts in which they take place; about how to relate the demands made of teachers to what they *actually* do - and what they feel about it.

This was - in a modest way - a genuine research experience. It involved a survey, through the literature, of what others had had to say of recent policies and practices relating to special educational needs in the UK; it called for a review and summary of the major pieces of legislation; and it required a drawing together and analysis of these informations, and their presentation in an emerging argument about the role of the special educator. The final result was published as a paper a year later in an international journal.

Chiefly, however, I feel that the experience met with a much-debated 'minimal definition' of research as 'sustained, systematic, self-critical enquiry made public' (Stenhouse, 1975, p.83). I shall return to this definition. I shall also, importantly, return to my paper, for a vital feature in my enquiry was the very role of teacher-as-researcher which I find implicit in a number of recent characterisations of the work of the inclusive educator.

---

[2] I use both these terms - 'special' and 'inclusive' - here because I see them not as opposed but as continually related, in keeping with Tony Booth's view of inclusion as essentially *processive* (see below). A distinctive feature of the Diploma/MEd (Inclusive Education) course is its commitment to promoting inclusive principles and practices; I take the position in this Unit that through self-critical reflection and action research, 'special' educators will necessarily develop an increasingly inclusive perspective.

ACTIVITY ONE
Before beginning work on this Study Unit, I should like you to give a few minutes thought to the impact of educational research on your own professional development. Make some notes on the following:

▪In the history of your own professional education and subsequent practice, which researchers and/or their works do you particularly remember? Why?
▪Which single piece of research during the last five years has had an impact on your and/or your institution's work?
▪In your view was this beneficial or otherwise?

▪Does your institution subscribe to m/any professional and/or research journals? Which? Are they much read/discussed? Do you personally subscribe?
▪Does your school/college actively encourage the discussion of research findings? How?
▪Does your school/college encourage the carrying out of research in whatever form?
▪Do you consider research to be a part of your job and professional development?

In a paper called 'On the Teacher as Researcher', Martin Hammersley (1993) collapses a number of criticisms of conventional educational research into the following accusations:
1.   That it is largely irrelevant to the practical concerns of teachers;
2.   That it is often invalid because it is separated from the object that it claims to understand: notably, the classroom practice of teachers;
3.   That it is undemocratic in that it allows the views of educational researchers to define the reality in which teachers are forced to work;
4.   That it amounts to a process of exploitation.

Now - and without too much reflection - 'score' each of these statements on a scale of 1 - 3, where 1 = agree, 2 = not sure/don't know and 3 = disagree.
Keep your answers to these questions by you as you work through the rest of the Study Unit; they may change!

CONTEMPORARY ISSUES IN EDUCATIONAL RESEARCH

EDUCATIONAL RESEARCH: A POOR BUY?

Some £70 million is estimated to be spent annually on educational research in the UK, and some 90% of this sum comes from government sources (Hargreaves 1996a; 1997; Bassey 1997). Although this figure represents less than 0.2% of the total government education spending, critics have pointed out that the same sum might buy employment for 2,800 teachers, or provide 70 secondary schools with a networked computer for each child (OFSTED, 1998, p,73). The question arises, then, as to whether research expenditure gives good value for money.

The debate really took off with David Hargreaves, Professor of Education at Cambridge University at the time of writing. In the Teacher Training Agency (TTA)[3] Annual Lecture in 1996, Hargreaves claimed simply - and boldly - that educational research generally is 'poor value for money in terms of improving the quality of education provided in schools' (Hargreaves 1996a, p.1). He argued that its relevance to improving classroom practice was minimal, and that it was frequently more occupied with arcane, in-house quarrels about methodology (p.3). A 'gap between researchers and practitioners' is a 'fatal flaw in educational research (p.3), for 'the researchers, not the practitioners... determine the agenda of educational research' (p.3) Allowing that *some* educational research may contribute to the raising of standards, or

---

[3] The Teacher Training Agency is - at the time of writing - a UK Governmental body whose purpose 'is to raise standards in schools by improving the quality of teacher training, teaching and school leadership, and by raising the status and esteem of the teaching profession'. There are many teachers in the UK who would argue with its effectiveness and effect in respect of these purposes.

increased educational opportunity, Hargreaves concluded nonetheless that much reported studies represent

> 'frankly second-rate educational research which does not make a serious contribution to fundamental theory or knowledge; which is irrelevant to practice; which is uncoordinated with any preceding or follow-up research; and which clutters up academic journals that virtually nobody reads.' (p.7)

Hargreaves' view is substantially borne out by the more recent 'Tooley Report' (OFSTED, 1998) of James Tooley and Doug Darby's review of 264 research articles from four 'top' UK educational journals; of these some 41 were analysed in detail, and were subjected to an analytic framework which was claimed to identify 'good practice' according to certain criteria. The details of these processes are of course important (and, equally, contestable; for many, the study provides a superb example of how *not* to carry out research!), but for the purposes of this Study Unit, I wish to report here only Tooley and Darby's gloomy conclusions:

> In terms of the 41 articles in the sub-sample [from the total of 264 articles], 15 are highlighted as showing good practice, with 26 highlighted as not satisfying criteria of good practice, in terms of certain dimensions of the analysis. Given the seriousness of many of these weaknesses, the tentative conclusion is that there are rather worrying tendencies in a *majority* of the articles surveyed...

> These conclusions may be disturbing, in particular in terms of the general health of the academic research community, and its potential influence in terms of the training and education of future teachers...
> (OFSTED, 1998, p.6)

And in his Foreword to the Report, Chris Woodhead[4] states baldly:

> Educational research is not making the contribution it should. Much that is published is, on this analysis, at best no more than an irrelevance and a distraction. To justify the expenditure of significant sums of public money, research must both illuminate issues of importance to teachers and exemplify the intellectual integrity upon which the pursuit of excellence ultimately depends.
>
> (*Ibid*, p.1)

What are the implications of such voices in the context of a research-based, in-service teacher education course such as ours? To answer this question, I shall first briefly consider the historical role of research in the creation of special education, and then sketch what I see as the distinctive contribution of the inclusive educator to improved practice. I shall do this by insisting that the inclusive educator is by definition occupied with an emancipatory programme which cannot be realised without research activity at various different levels.

RESEARCH IN SPECIAL AND INCLUSIVE EDUCATION

What is the peculiar relevance of these developments for special and inclusive education? To answer this question, I shall first present a brief overview of research traditions in the area of *special* education, before characterising a distinctive role for research in the development of *inclusive* education.

---

[4] Chris Woodhead is - at the time of writing - Her Majesty's Chief Inspector of Schools. As with the TTA, many teachers are critical of his influence on the development of education in the UK.

The purposes of modern (that is to say, post-1944) special education are to be found in the need to remove responsibility for the 'difficult to teach' from mainstream schools and their teachers. You will remember from Unit 1 that these purposes were easily fuelled by a medically-derived notion of *deficit*, built on profound traditions of research in a *positivist* framework; such research, operating on the assumption that 'the methodological procedures of natural science may be directly applied' (Giddens, 1974, p.3), has no problems in seeing its *subjects as objects* and (learning) *difficulties as deficits*. Such ideology and its programme (of research) derive reflexively from the origins of special education in medical and then psycho-medical attitudes to ab/normality.

What was an interesting consequence of this *hegemony* of deficit-driven attitudes was that the special educator entered a world of ready-made expertise and attribution; children were known in the first instance by their failure in one way or another, and these failures could be more or less precisely described by the terms and tools of the clinician. One of the things which made special education 'special' - and, indeed, unique in educational institutional practice - was the existence of technologies for identification, diagnosis and remediation which directly informed pedagogy; there was no parallel to this in other, 'non-special' practice.

This is not to say, of course, that 'special' education always proceeded in such a technically-precise way (and there is much evidence to suggest that a great deal of it was sloppy; see Brennan, 1982, for example). But the point I wish to emphasise is how *received categories* have always conditioned 'special' practice; historically, disabled pupils and people have been identified in official and professional discourses in ways which separate *and* marginalise them:

'They' are identified by what they cannot do,
by what is 'wrong' with them. They have been
- over time - the *lunatics*, the *idiots*, the
'mentally-handicapped', the '(educationally)
sub-normal, the *spastics*, the *cripples* and -
even - the *level-one child*. The point is that *we*
know who *they* are; they are conspicuous
because their world is set about with a
particularly forceful categorical thinking.
(adapted from Clough and Barton, 1995, p.9)

During the last thirty or so years, such categorical thinking has been forcefully challenged by sociologists and others (Tomlinson, 1982; Barton and Tomlinson 1984). At the same time, the work of curriculum theorists (Stenhouse, 1975; Carr and Kemmis, 1986) and certain learning theorists (see Macdonald, 1979) have contributed to an emerging view of learning/difficulty as essentially situational, as functions of socially constructed events and meanings. In this climate, positivist categorically-led research is seen as at best reductionist and, in any event, as perpetuating a disabling ideology which sees '...the problem which disabled people face as being caused by their own impairments' (Oliver, 1992, p.108).

In tandem with UK policy developments which re-conceived of learning difficulties in a situated and relative way (Warnock, 1978; HMSO, 1981), there were many calls for an empirical research in special education which would treat more sensitively of the matter and experience of learning difficulty. Schindele (1985) for example, cites as a major priority in respect of research objectives the exploration of meanings, of subjective definitions and complex relationships; citing Wolf and Tymitz (1976) he says that research must '...aim at understanding actualities, social realities and human perceptions'; of primary importance is the '...understanding [of] human behaviour from the subject's own frame of reference' (Bogdan and Biklen, 1982).

Schindele's (*op.cit.*) call for 'more adequate and more systematic application of qualitative research methodology' is taken up in the same collection of papers by Corrie and Zaklukievicz (*ibid.*) whose quotation from Eggleston (1974) is instructive: '...the 'scientific' conception of the everyday world that has to be adopted in order to act in a scientific way is at variance with the subtle, shifting and often covert everyday conceptions of the world and the responses to it that are at the heart of what is being studied; ... the dissonance between methodology and phenomena in education has in consequence become more manifest...'

But it remains arguable whether research in special/inclusive education has really broken out of its positivist origins (and you must judge the extent of this from your own reading of the current literature). There is, however, a further and key strand to current thinking and developments which arises chiefly from the voice of disabled researchers, and their concern with emancipatory research.

INCLUSION, EMANCIPATION AND RESEARCH

If the dominant voices in special education have been - and continue to be - infected with positivist and medico-psychological models of difference, there is a number of emerging *alternative* voices struggling to be heard. Here is one such, which points up quite particularly the role which (academic) researchers play in sustaining subject-object relations in enquiry:

By our insistence upon the use of certain 'professional' textual practices, we do not allow ourselves to be influenced in our identities, as the academic professionals we are. Thus, no matter how benevolent we may be towards those we study - no matter how concerned with 'their' liberation, with their betterment, with preventing 'their' victimisation, etc - the fact is that 'we' do not make sense of 'their' lives in 'their' terms. 'We' *do not even* make sense of 'their' lives 'with them'. While what they say is treated as data, they themselves are not treated seriously as being able to speak the truth about their own lives; their claims do not pass 'our' institutional tests.

(Shotter, 1993, p.48)

Shotter's indictment of various research positions is a powerful reminder of the power relations of research production which polarises researcher and researched and which ultimately therefore maintains - even strengthens - institutional inequalities. In the case of disability research, this argument has been variously articulated by researchers who are themselves disabled (see, particularly, Abberley,1992; Barnes, 1992; Oliver, 1992). At the heart of their concerns is an insistence on a research process which is *democratic, transformative* and - above all - *emancipatory*.

ACTIVITY TWO
You should now read 'Developing an emancipatory research agenda: possibilities and dilemmas' (Barton, 1998). During and after your reading, consider the following :

Barton outlines a highly political agenda; do you agree that the role of the researcher should be seen in this way?

Can people ever really 'empower themselves'?

Barton's focus is chiefly on disability research; to what extent are his arguments applicable to other instances of difficulty, children with Emotional and Behavioural Difficulties, for example? Or learners whose powers of articulation are apparently limited? Should they 'have a say'? And how should we 'access' them?

Although Barton does not focus explicitly on it, it must be clear from his paper that teachers must be equally involved in such emancipatory research. How can this be achieved? In the next section, I shall firstly outline some principles of teacher research before indicating the specific and *necessary* role of teacher research in the realisation of inclusive education.

THE TEACHER AS RESEARCHER

Arguably the most important figure in the development of a teacher- and action-research movement in the UK was Lawrence Stenhouse. His work was an essentially liberal and humanist project; at its centre is a model of the learner - understood equally as student, as teacher, as anyone wherever in the educational process - *actually and actively creating knowledge in real situations*; and just as situations change by definition, this knowledge changes, is developed, refined, or even replaced. In any event, it is always contestable and open to debate (Stenhouse 1975).

A clear and operational consequence of this view is that learners - again broadly defined - need to be brought face to face with their practices and processes, in order to develop a critical self-consciousness. As Hammersley (1993) interprets Stenhouse, 'we are constrained by assumptions and habits built up in the past and ... it is the business of education to make us freer and more creative'(p.213). Such a view leads Stenhouse to a call for:

> - the commitment to systematic questioning of one's own teaching as a basis for development;
> - the commitment and the skills to study one's own teaching;
> - the concern to question and to test theory in practice by the use of those skills;
> - readiness to allow others to observe your work and to discuss it with them on an honest, open basis.
>
> (Stenhouse, 1975, p.144)

ACTIVITY THREE

Let us look at an example of a reported piece of teacher-research. There are, of course, thousands to choose from, and each will be unique. The following, however, may be a 'good' example, not least because it was deemed suitable for publication in the prestigious British Educational Research Journal published by the British Educational Research Association.

In brief, the 'story' of this paper tells of how the author, Kay Chiswell was a teacher in the early 1990s when she enrolled on a course at the University of Birmingham School of Education; here she was encouraged to 'reflect upon my teaching in a critical way, to analyse my strengths and weaknesses, and by implementing action steps, provide the means of altering or improving my teaching practices'. (p. 413)

This led her consciously to change her teaching from its apparently 'formal, didactic' style to a more 'progressive' one, and she writes:

'This first analysis of my teaching practices, although late in my career, prompted me to change the situation in which I taught and, hopefully, the learning opportunities of my class'. (p. 415)

Her decisions were taken:
subject to two safeguards: (a) they were made as a result of critical educational research, and (b) they were guided by a commitment to the well-being of the children'. (p. 415)

They led to immediately noticeable effects:

With the change from formal methods of teaching and learning, the noise level rose and I had difficulty in accepting this at first. I assumed that talking, moving about and general classroom noise indicated a lack of learning'. (p. 415)

However, on examining the taped evidence which appeared to suggest improved fluency and articulacy, she changed this view, and thus was able to justify the radical change of her teaching methods.

Let's now look at this paper and its evidence in more detail and critically examine its claims to be 'sustained, systematic self-conscious enquiry made public' (Stenhouse, op cit)

Read Chiswell, K. (1995) 'How is action research helping to develop my role as a communicator?'

When you have read the paper, consider these questions:

What exactly does the author mean by 'critical educational research' (and what exactly is that research)?
What evidence is there that the children's learning did actually improve?
How is this evidence tested and justified?
Who benefited from this study and how? Did the author? Did her pupils? And did you, the reader?
This last question is vital, and a reminder that research worthy of the name must ultimately, persuade.

PROCESSES OF TEACHER RESEARCH AND INCLUSIVE EDUCATION

I will argue simply that the nature of inclusive education *positively requires* programmes of teacher- and action-research. At its simplest, this is because inclusive principles and practices share with the principles and practices of teacher research a central concern with *informed participation* and *institutional transformation*.

Returning to the principles of teacher research, Carr and Kemmis identify the *reflective* and *critical* task of research enquiry:

> the primary task for any research activity concerned to adopt a scientific approach to educational problems is to emancipate them from their dependence on habit and tradition by providing them with the skills and resources that will enable them to reflect upon and examine critically the inadequacies of different conceptions of educational practice... This does not mean that 'practical' ways of thinking must be abandoned in favour of some 'theoretical' mode of thought. What is being abandoned is an unreflective attitude so that a more critical, scientific attitude can be adopted towards established educational creeds. Hence, science does not *replace* existing theories of educational practice so much as *improve* them, by subjecting the beliefs and justifications which sustain them to criticism. For it is only by so challenging current educational certainties that the interpretations and judgements of educators will become more coherent and less dependent on the prejudices and dogma that permeate unreflective educational thinking.
>
> (Carr and Kemmis 1986, p.124)

Such a view of research process and outcome is radically different from those of Hargreaves (*op.cit.*) and OFSTED (*op.cit.*) which we looked at earlier. And, in particular, Carr and Kemmis' theorisation of research has a quite specific relevance in the context of inclusion; for, as we have seen, 'special' education and research have their roots in *traditions of exclusive thinking which still deeply infect current practices*. And it is the task of the critical researcher to expose these traditional influences in the attitudes and institutions of which they are expressions; to hold them up to critical enquiry and evaluate their moral and political effects.

This research *process* is again wholly one with the inclusive project - itself a *process* without conclusion. For, as Booth (1998) has it, 'inclusion' is essentially about the *process* 'of *increasing* the participation of students in the curricula, cultures and communities of neighbourhood mainstream educational institutions'; it is at the same time about the *process* of *reducing* the exclusion of [those students]' (my italics).

For Barton, similarly, inclusive education is '... about how, where and why, and with what consequences, we educate *all* pupils' (Barton, 1997, p. 234). Such 'Education for all... involves a serious commitment to the task of identifying, challenging and contributing to the removal of injustices' (*ibid.*). The project, then, carries its own research agenda in which *all* are involved, and whose methodology is given with the nature of the problem:

> Inclusive education is about responding to diversity; it is about listening to unfamiliar voices, being open, empowering all members and about celebrating 'difference' in dignified ways. From this perspective, the goal is not to leave anyone out of school. Inclusive education is about learning to live with one another.' (*Ibid*; my italics)

ACTIVITY FOUR

You should now read 'New Directions in Special Educational Needs Research', Vulliamy, G. & Webb, R. (1992). Although this paper pre-dates the more recent discourse about inclusion, it nevertheless provides a coherent overview of most of the issues discussed so far. (You should at some point during the course look at the book as a whole, as it contains some nine reports of teacher-research carried out as part of a higher-degree programme at the University of York.)

THE INCLUSIVE RESEARCHER

At the beginning of this Study Unit, I wrote about a research experience arising from an attempt to represent to European colleagues something of the state of UK teacher education in the area of special educational needs. I return to this here finally, because this was not merely a 'research' experience in itself, but one whose content and outcomes actually re-affirmed the research role of the special/inclusive educator.

The paper posed the question: What implications do changes in the statutory role of the special educator have for teacher education and professional development programmes? The article looked at current policy in the UK, and at a number of ways in which commentators have seen the increasing complication of the role of the special/inclusive educator. In particular, the role of the Special Educational Needs Co-Ordinator (SENCO) is defined in the Code of Practice in terms of a responsibility for:

- the day to day operation of the school's special educational needs policy;
- liaising with and advising fellow teachers;
- contributing to the in-service training of staff;
- maintaining the school's special educational needs register and overseeing the records of all pupils with special educational needs;
- co-ordinating provision for children with special educational needs;
- liaising with parents of children with special educational needs;
- liaising with external agencies including the educational psychology service and other support agencies, medical and social services and voluntary bodies.

(DfEE, 1994, para 2.14[/11])

My paper concludes that most of these activities can only be carried out successfully with a 'research attitude'.

This is to ask: how can you know whether your judgement in each of the above duties is sound without subjecting it to the opinions of others - students, parents, teachers, governors and so on? And those of people who may have systematically studied that area? And, above all, without wondering - at least - about why you are interested in and doing these things; about what, that is, your own ideology means?

Thus the paper concludes that the curriculum for the professional development of the special/inclusive educator is essentially a *critical* one. The generic elements of such a programme are easy - if daunting - to state, but widely and deeply ranging; I suggest that the special/inclusive educator needs a training, but much more an education in

- **pedagogy** (including appropriate psychological knowledge and technique);
- **curriculum** (including analytic differentiation skills);
- **administration** (including legal and financial knowledge and skills);
- **management** (including staff development and training skills);

and, under-pinning all of these,

- **research** (including 'action' programmes as well as access to/familiarity with published studies).

(Clough, 1998; amended)

DEVELOPING A RESEARCH ATTITUDE

Stenhouse characterised research as 'sustained, systematic, self-critical enquiry made public' (1975, p.75). Of course, how long it is 'sustained', quite how it is 'systematic', the nature of its 'self-critical' tone and the forum in which it is 'made public' may vary widely from one enquiry to the next. But Stenhouse's 'minimal definition' serves equally for the large-scale, funded project and the small-scale teacher research enquiry. At its simplest, the whole point of such enquiry is *to make the familiar strange*; so to look at the daily phenomena of educational practice that their essential features are exposed, and their meaning considered against other settings, other views, others' insights.

Thus *becoming critical* is about bringing to routine practices questions that we do not normally ask of ourselves; it is also about comparing our answers to those of other researchers. Viewed in this way, teacher- and action-research may very well be focused on what we do every day for a living - but what distinguishes it from that routine professional practice is its contextualisation in the work and the insights of others. Thus, for example, the literature review is ultimately no more than an attempt to locate a particular study in the fields, traditions and findings of like enquiry. The review will reveal equally how others have answered our particular questions and in what ways those particular questions remain to be answered: that 'surplus' of question over answer provides the justification for the study.

But Stenhouse emphasises not merely the *critical* but the *self-critical*, and this dimension has a particular relevance in the context of inclusive education. I have argued above that in this context the teacher-researcher has a quite particular - an *extra* - responsibility by virtue of a moral and political commitment to inclusive principles, and to practices fundamentally concerned with change. Thus teacher-research in the area must at all times be self-conscious in its examination of the assumptions and thought-shapes that are at work in the enquiry.

Such self-consciousness may be best illustrated by reference to a set of studies entitled *Making Difficulties* (Clough and Barton, 1995), in which researchers reflected on their own 'insertion' in their various research studies. In asking them to do this, we provided a list of questions for them to answer in one way or another. These were:

> What assumptions about SEN/disability do I have which are inevitably present in the way I conceive of the study?
> What specific questions - in the light of these - am I asking in this particular study, and which events and circumstances prompted them, and gave them a particular urgency?
> Why and how did these assumptions, questions and circumstances suggest or require the particular methods which I chose? What assumptions about 'how the world operates' - and how we can know it - are given with these methods? Why, then, are they particularly suitable for investigating the phenomena in question?
> How did the process of my research change or qualify my assumptions? In what ways am I changed by the research?
> And in what ways is the community's understanding changed by what I have achieved?
> (Adapted from Clough and Barton, 1995, p.3)

Although these were questions addressed to (and by) professional researchers, it should be clear that they can be applied to and by any researcher. (They are, in fact, no more than the fundamental questions of a *methodology* - rather than method - whose task is to uncover and justify assumptions as far and as practicably as possible, and in so doing to locate the claims which the research makes in the traditions of enquiry which guide it.)

'MANY URGENT VOICES'

Action-research is essentially about change. As Carr and Kemmis (1986) say, it can

> ... establish conditions under which it can identify and expose those aspects of the social order which frustrate rational change, and provide a basis for action to overcome irrationality, injustice and deprivation. It does so by creating conditions in which the self-critical communities of action researchers commit themselves to rational communication, just and democratic decision-making and access to an interesting and satisfying life for all.'
>
> (Carr and Kemmis, 1986, p.197)

The final reading in this Unit amplifies the roles and responsibilities of the researcher which are implicit in Carr and Kemmis' account. It is taken from the conclusion to *Making Difficulties*, and reflects some of the insights reported in that collection.

> **ACTIVITY FIVE**
>
> **Self-critical action research is without doubt an unsettling and frequently disturbing process - both for the researcher and (often) for her/his institution. You should now read *'Conclusion; many urgent voices'*. (Clough and Barton, 1995).**
>
> **Look again at your notes from Activity 1. Have your views changed at all? In particular, to what extent do you identify with the each of the roles we outline?**

CONCLUSION

In this Unit I hope to have dis-covered and rehearsed the key, organic and radical role which teacher-research can play in transforming education generally, and in realising inclusive principles in action. I have suggested that there is a particularly powerful synergy to be found in bringing together the projects of action research and inclusive practice, since both *methodologies* start from a questioning of easy assumptions, and both seek change characterised by quite urgent moral and political values. Such research has ethical as well as clearly utilitarian justification. Of course, it is not easy.

REFERENCES

Abberley, P. (1992) 'Counting us out: a discussion of the OPCS disability surveys' in *Disability, Handicap and Society,* Vol 7, No 2, pp 139-156.

Barnes, C. (1992) 'Qualitative Research: Valuable or Irrelevant?' in *Disability, Handicap and Society*, Vol 7, No 2, pp 115 - 124.

Barton, L. and Tomlinson S. (1984) (Eds) *Special Education and Social Interests,* London: Croom Helm.

Barton, L. (1997) 'Inclusive Education: romantic, subversive or realistic?' in *International Journal of Inclusive Education,* Vol 1, No 3, pp 231-242.

Barton, L. (1998) 'Developing an emancipatory research agenda: possibilities and dilemmas' in Clough, P. and Barton, L. (Eds) *Articulating with Difficulty: research voices in inclusive education,* London: PCP/BERA New Dialogues.

Bassey, M. (1997) 'Annual expenditure on educational research in the UK' in *Research Intelligence,* No, 59, February pp. 2 -3.

Booth, T. (1998) 'Embracing the faith: including the community?'. Paper given at *Inclusion in the City* symposium, BERA, Belfast Aug.

Brennan, W. (1982) *Special Education in Mainstream Schools - The Search for Quality,* Stratford-upon-Avon: National Council for Special Education.

Carr, W. and Kemmis, S. (1986) *Becoming Critical,* Lewes: Falmer.

Chiswell, K. (1995) 'How is action research helping to develop my role as a communicator?' in *British Educational Research Journal,* Vol 21, No 3, pp 413-420.

Clough, P. (1998) 'Balancing Acts: policy agenda for teacher education and special educational needs' in *Journal of Education for Teaching,* Vol 24, No 1, pp 63-71.

Clough, P. and Barton, L. (Eds) (1995) *Making Difficulties: research and the construction of special educational need,* London: PCP.

Corrie, M. and Zaklukievicz, S. (1985) 'Qualitative research and case-study approaches: an introduction' in Hegarty, S. and Evans, P. (Eds) *Research and Evaluation Methods in Special Education,* Windsor: NFER-Nelson.

DfEE (1994) *The Code of Practice,* London: HMSO.

Eggleston, J. (1974) *Contemporary Research in the Sociology of Education,* London: Methuen.

Giddens, A. (Ed) (1974) *Positivism and Sociology,* London: Heinemann.

Hammersley, M. (1993) 'On the Teacher as Researcher' in Hammersley, M. (Ed) *Educational Research: current issues,* London: PCP/Open University.

Hargreaves, D. (1996) *Teaching as a Research-Based Profession: possibilities and prospects; the Teacher Training Agency Annual Lecture 1996,* mimeo.

Hargreaves, D. (1997) 'In defence of research for evidence-based teaching: a rejoinder to Martyn Hammersley' in *British Educational Research Journal,* Vol 23, No 2.

HMSO (1981) *The Education Act,* London: HMSO.

Macdonald, M. (1979) *Children's Minds,* London: Fontana.

OFSTED (1998) *Educational Research: a critique,* London: OFSTED.

Oliver, M. (1992) 'Changing the social relations of research production' in *Disability, Handicap and Society,* Vol 7, No 2, pp 101-114.

Schindele. R. (1985) 'Research methodology in special education: a framework approach to special problems and solutions' in Hegarty, S. and Evans, P. (Eds) *Research and Evaluation Methods in Special Education,* Windsor: NFER Nelson.

Shotter, J. (1993) *Cultural Politics and Everyday Life,* Buckingham: Open University Press.

Stenhouse, L. (1975) *An Introduction to Curriculum Research and Development,* London: Heinemann.

Tomlinson, S. (1982) *A Sociology of Special Education,* London: RKP.

Vulliamy, G. and Webb, R. (Eds) (1992*) Teacher Research and Special Educational Needs,* London: David Fulton.

Warnock (1978) *Report of the Warnock Commission,* London: HMSO.

Wolf, R. and Tymitz, B. (1976) 'Ethnography and reading: matching inquiry mode to process' in *Reading Research Quarterly,* Sept. pp 38-56.

UNIT TEN

DEVELOPING FUTURE AGENDAS

FELICITY ARMSTRONG AND LEN BARTON

This book has explored a number of important ideas from a range of diverse perspectives and starting points. In this final Unit we will try and link some of these ideas to a consideration of the development of future agendas relating to research, practice and policy making. These agendas are not different and separate but relate to each other in important ways, underlining the necessity of establishing closer exchanges between all those who have an interest in education - including those involved as learners - so that we can gain a better understanding of different issues and perspectives relating to the struggle for an inclusive society. This is one of the main concerns of this book.

One question that emerges in many of the contributions to this book is the importance of understanding the relationship between dominant discourses, values and practices surrounding education and differences in treatment and opportunities experienced by different groups in society. Every-day inequalities that permeate education, reflect and reproduce social relations and inequalities in wider society and across cultures. At the same time, they are open to mediation and to contestation at many levels. Policies that are made at central government level can be re-interpreted and reworked at local government level. Individual schools or groups of schools can 'make' policies of their own by adopting positions on equal opportunities which subvert ethnocentric curricula or excluding pedagogies, as well as by refusing to allocate resources in ways that are unjust. Teachers can subvert policies made elsewhere through the practices and attitudes they foster in their classrooms. Finally, students can themselves challenge policies and practices, subverting and transforming them in both the individual and collective experience of learning.

Conditions and relations in society are constantly changing, old patterns, agendas and allegiances are broken and new ones emerge. So when we talk about 'the system', 'the state' or even 'education' we are not referring to static conditions and relations, but complex, ever-changing sets of circumstances, groupings, interests and values. Within this flux and confusion, there are some certainties, though, which can be summarised as follows:

- In different societies there are dominant *cultural understandings* about the interests and groups that education systems serve through the values, structures and processes of selection and partitioning which permeate them.

- These cultural understandings ignore the paradox of deploring violations of human rights that are culturally recognised, while implicitly accepting those that are hidden or regarded as 'natural' within 'ones own' society.

- Understandings and recognition of human rights are uneven. That is why a policy of apartheid is publicly deplored in many societies, yet in those same societies thousands of disabled children are placed in segregated schools.

- Processes and procedures relating to the selecting in and the selecting out of different groups of students are seen as natural, being embedded in social attitudes and cultural practice. Far from the inclusion of all children in common educational and social settings being seen as an ordinary right, in many contexts such a demand is regarded as impractical, hopelessly idealistic, unrealistic, disturbing.

- The categories and labels that are assigned to people on the basis of perceived differences in performance, appearance or behaviour depend upon social and cultural variables and benchmarks of 'normality' and, as such, are socially constructed rather than being 'true' descriptors of individuals.

- Discourse is critical in shaping social worlds and people's understanding of their own - and others' - roles and relations within them.

- Dominant ways of talking about 'policy' as rational, made by government and handed down for implementation by elected representatives and public servants obscure the complex and idiosyncratic ways in which things come to be as they are. This illusion of rationality and purpose is disempowering because it confuses perceptions about the possibility and necessity of individuals, groups and local communities bringing about change through their own actions.

- The struggle for inclusive education is part of a wider struggle to bring about an inclusive society in which all individuals and groups enjoy full and equal membership. As such, it involves asking questions and making demands that are disturbing. because they challenge the familiar and the way in which our own societies are organised.

In our introduction we said that while the contributors to this book do not share a common perspectives on all aspects of the issues raised, we do agree that it is 'essential to identify and understand those factors that make 'difference' so significant, that oppression, exclusion and discrimination become basic features of the social relations and conditions of a society'. And we agree that this is not just a question concerning individuals and attitudes but is fundamentally concerned with the institutionalisation of inequalities in society.

The 'institutions' which make up education systems include not just school and college buildings, curricula, assessment procedures, budgets, school development plans and written policies. They are not just the preserve of educational planners, administrators, advisors, researchers, teachers and students. They are an organic part of communities and of wider society. As such, what happens in education is crucial in terms of the values and practices it develops and sustains.

Agendas concerning education are - and have to be - the concern of the whole of society. They also have to recognise that in establishing agendas, those participating in debates on education and inclusion frequently find themselves defending conflicting principles and perceptions of the way forward. In this situation it is hardly surprising that there is a tendency for those involved to retrench themselves behind sloganeering and even invective! Academics are often accused of pontificating from ivory towers and wasting money on irrelevant research. Professionals have frequently been cited as defending their own professional and career interests (and hence standing in the way of change). Policy makers and school governors are seen as concerned with agendas relating to budgets and school performance tables. Parents' voices are rarely heard and students themselves are largely excluded from debates about the kind of education they would like. Activists in the Disability Movement - while making a major contribution in bringing disability and human rights issues to public attention - are generally marginalised in the media and in debates orchestrated by central government. In spite of these major difficulties, attitudes are changing. Increasingly policy makers, teachers and parents are looking for examples of inclusive schools and practices as part of their search for new ideas and practices.

The development of new agendas which will be effective and creative in moving towards inclusive education and an inclusive society, rests upon *establishing connections* between different perspectives and understandings. The study of history and of different societies and cultures through the perspectives of those belonging to them is particularly rich in opportunities for making connections and cross-cultural comparisons. These can offer us new ways of looking at our own societies and present creative alternatives to what we have always seen as 'inevitable', 'natural' or impossible to change.

Part of the struggle is about building dialogues between different groups. This means working together on different projects within a culture of mutual curiosity and respect.

What might this look like in practice? One example close to our own experience can be found in the projects based on collaboration and critical enquiry carried out by students in Singapore, Hong Kong, Trinidad and Tobago and in England (who come from at least fourteen different countries), who have enrolled on our distance learning Diploma and Masters Inclusive Education programme based at the University of Sheffield.

Other examples can be found in which LEAs and individual schools, teachers, parents and members of the local community in the United Kingdom have collaborated to try and bring about change in the kind of education children and young people are offered. The experience of such projects needs to be disseminated, discussed, questioned and known about.

Any future agenda must be built upon an understanding of the importance of listening to others, sharing ideas and making connections. We hope that this book will contribute to this aim.